Beginning A
New Pastorate

Creative Leadership Series

Lyle E. Schaller, Editor

Beginning A New Pastorate

Robert G. Kemper

Abingdon   Nashville

BEGINNING A NEW PASTORATE

Copyright © 1978 by Robert G. Kemper

Library of Congress Cataloging in Publication Data

KEMPER, ROBERT G
  Beginning a new pastorate.

  (Creative leadership series)
  1. Clergy-Office. 2. Clergy—Appointment, call, and elec-
tion. 3. Clergymen's families. 4. Pastoral theology. I. Title.
BV660.2.K46   253'.2   77-18055

ISBN 0-687-02750-0

MANUFACTURED BY THE PARTHENON PRESS AT
NASHVILLE, TENNESSEE, UNITED STATES OF AMERICA

FOR MY MOTHER AND FATHER

They had five churches in my youth.
Four times I hated moving
because I loved each place so much.

Foreword

"I wonder how it feels for a minister to move into a new pastorate in a strange community."

"Yes, and I wonder how his wife and children feel about pulling up roots in one community and moving to a new church."

"We seem to be losing more members out the back door than we take in through the front door. In looking over the records it appears that between one third and one half of our new members become inactive within three years after they join. I wonder what we could do to improve how we assimilate new members."

"I saw in a recent survey of pastors that one of the points of the greatest discontent and frustration among ministers was the management of their time. Sometimes I feel that is also one of my biggest problems."

"Other congregations seem to find enough lay volunteers to staff their program. What are we doing, or not doing, that makes it so difficult for us to fill all the leadership positions in our church?"

"There certainly has been a lot of research carried out in recent years on how people learn and on better teaching methods. I wonder what they have discovered that we could apply or adapt to the educational ministry of our church."

These are representative of the questions, expressions of frustration, and concerns heard repeatedly in talking with church leaders, both lay and clergy. This book by Robert G. Kemper is the first volume in the Creative Leadership Series. This series of paperbound books is a response to these and similar questions and concerns. This first volume is filled with insights, ideas, and suggestions for the minister about to begin a new pastorate and for the lay leaders in the congregation seeking or about to welcome a new pastor. Every year one congregation out of three bids farewell to a pastor or an associate minister or an ordained program specialist. When that vacant position is filled it means a series of adjustments for the newly arrived pastor, for the congregation, for the minister's family, for the close friends of the former pastor, and for the community. In this volume Bob Kemper reflects on these adjustments and offers scores of suggestions for making this a more creative experience for everyone.

The second volume in this series is focused on the neglected process of assimilating new members into the life and fellowship of the worshiping congregation. If one looks at the actual experiences of thousands of new adult members, it appears that in many congregations it is easier to join that congregation than it is to be welcomed and accepted into the fellowship circle. This second volume is filled with creative suggestions on how a congregation can be more effective in receiving and assimilating new members.

Subsequent volumes in this series will focus on the care and feeding of lay volunteers in the church, on the management of time, on the creativity in Christian education and the teaching ministry, and on related subjects of interest to leaders in the churches.

We trust this series of books on creative Christian leadership will be helpful both to ministers and to church members as they respond in faithfulness and obedience to the call of Christ to labor in his vineyard.

Lyle E. Schaller
Yokefellow Institute
Richmond, Indiana

Preface

A church is a church is a church. Ministry is ministry is ministry. Moving is moving is moving.

Baloney! None of those is true.

Yet in the minds of countless clergy those beliefs are operative. This book will attempt to jar those conceptions. There is another way, a better way to conceive of churches, ministry, and moving. Clergy have an itinerant tradition. They come and go. This book supposes that those comings and goings have special meanings, require special understandings, and promise special satisfactions.

In the strict sense of the term, this is not a how-to-do-it book. No one knows that. Especially, no one knows how you should do it. Rather, this book advocates a process. It is a for-instance of how that process might be applied to the change of pastorates. The name of the process is intentionality. Its tools are negotiation and freedom. Its expected ends are trust and growth.

This is a book and not an encyclopedia. It would take an encyclopedia to cover all the sorts and conditions of ministry. Of necessity the book has a narrow model. It supposes that the reader is male and is moving for the second or third time to a single pastorate church. The author is well aware that not all clergy are male, that the reader may not yet be ordained, or may be a veteran of many moves, or that a staff position may be in his future. You, thus, will have to be responsible for translating this work into your own terms.

Further, I have assumed a normal motivation to move. I do not even know what that is, but I do know what it is not. It is not a desperate situation in which one simply must leave his present pastorate and move to whatever is available to him. That is a very special circumstance and needs its own book. This book suggests ways to help avoid that unpleasantness.

The specific situations of every move are unique. Those who move, where they move to, and the manner in which they do so may offer a near-infinite range of nuances. Nevertheless, it is my hope that the reader—whether man or woman, young or old, eager or desperate—will find here ideas, concepts, and approaches that can be adopted and adapted to his particular, unique circumstances.

As I wrote these words I found myself using the second person pronoun *you*. I do not know who "you" are. But in the final analysis that does not matter. You know who you are, and you know what approach you want to take in your new pastorate. What I offer you are some thoughts about beginning. The merit of these thoughts depends upon what you make of them. I have narrowed the perception of the you to whom I am speaking in order to clarify the intentional process. My narrow concept will be broadened as your thoughts are fused with mine.

Contents

I

Keys: What It Means to Move

In the Car

This is a strange day for me. I am driving on the interstate with my family. We are on our way to our new home in a new town and, for me, new work. The kids have finally grown weary of squabbling in the back seat, my wife is quiet in her own thoughts, and for the first time in many days I have a few minutes to think.

The physical facts of moving are like the physical facts of pregnancy: The pain is both unbearable and forgettable. If human beings remembered the agony of loading all their belongings into a moving van, they would never move! I never realized how much stuff we had accumulated until I saw it all scattered over our front lawn. I never would have been a good missionary if I had had to move my family halfway around the

17

world! Fortunately, this move is not halfway around the world, but nevertheless it is to a new world for us. My head is in a swirl. How many times can you say good-bye? How many promises of keeping in touch can you make? How many tears can a family shed? We have all shed so many tears that we have had to drink more water just to replenish the tear glands! Further, we are all tired, just plain exhausted. We are bushed from all the physical work of moving; but more, we are wrung out from the experience of leaving.

I sure appreciated Bill Reace's call to me yesterday. It was very thoughtful of him to let us know that the new house was cleaned and waiting for us, with a supply of groceries in the cabinets. That was really nice. I am also glad I made a reservation at a motel with a swimming pool for tonight. Eddie, Ginny, and Betsy would not have gotten in the car to leave this morning if I hadn't reminded them that we would be in a pool soon.

I don't blame them. Moving is hard on the family. Eddie was just finding his way in high school. Ginny was working through the adolescent crisis in junior high. Betsy loved walking to her grade school in the neighborhood with her friends. And, of course, Margie really hated leaving this place—where a child was born, where she knew so many people, where she had become comfortable in her own role. And I—well, sometimes I feel like the world's worst villain. I brought all this suffering on my dear ones. But, on the other hand, sometimes I am so excited about the prospects of my new work. I have so many ideas I want to try. I have a great challenge and opportunity. So many things are going to be new, different, and better. What was it Paul Tillich used to say in seminary about "the ambiguities of existence"? Well, I feel the ambiguities of existence.

I sure had a strange sensation when I put the keys in the car to start this trip. I noticed that my key case—which always bulged with house keys, church keys, file keys, desk keys: keys whose use I had long forgotten—was nearly empty. The only keys I had were the car keys. What a sinking feeling! Possessions do not mean that much to me; honest, they do not. But somehow that key case symbolized all that I was giving up. When we arrive in Western Springs, Illinois, the first thing I am going to do is put some new keys in my pocket.

Keys are important in moving. There are symbolic and substantive keys. They open doors and they secure closed doors. In this chapter on what it means to move, we want to look at the keys of moving, what they represent, and how they are used. It is proper and very important to begin with a discussion of what it means to move. Most people move several times in their lives; it is part of the American nomadic tradition. But the focus here is on ministers and their moving. That, too, has a long tradition, e.g., "By faith Abraham obeyed when he was called to go out to a place which he was to receive as an inheritance; and he went out, not knowing where he was to go" (Heb. 11:8 RSV).

Beginning a New Pastorate

What Is Moving?

Moving is the disruption of familiar communal patterns.

Physical place and personal identity are interrelated. In time, who we are and where we are form an abiding bond. How often in meeting strangers one of the first points of contact is the exchange of information about our respective locations. Where are you from? is a key identity. Moving, which is a change of location, involves very personal identity changes.

Further, we associate meanings with place. Many traveling vacations are pilgrimages to historic places. To be in Washington, D.C., is to be in a place where many significant events in our larger lives have happened. In the case of a place of residency, we associate many events of personal significance with the particularities of place. This is where we live. This is where my child was born. This is where my mother is buried. When we move we change our primary location, and a simple fact of experience begins: Significant places of significant happenings are "back home." (As you make a move, you may want to be conscious of your own language in this matter. How long will it be before you stop referring to the place where you used to live as "back home"? Home is where you are now. See how long it takes for you to start living in the present.) You will change your language about "back home" when you begin to associate significant events with your present location.

Moving dislocates you from place. A second dimension is the disruption of your network of

ERRATA

Beginning a New Pastorate
by Robert G. Kemper

The paragraph beginning at the bottom of page 20 should read as follows to line 4 on page 21:

Moving dislocates you from place. A second dimension is the disruption of your network of interpersonal relationships. The primary experience of moving is anonymity: No one knows your name. Over and over you must introduce yourself and be introduced.

Lines following are correct as printed.

introduced. That process never ends as we continually widen our circle of acquaintances, but in the Over and over you must introduce yourself and be introduced. That process never ends as we continually widen our circle of acquaintances, but in the experience of moving it begins afresh, often totally and completely. Moving makes you a stranger, an outsider, even an intruder. The other side of the experience is that moving makes you a dropout, a willing disassociate, maybe even a traitor to your former network of personal associates. By leaving one network for another, you betray the one you leave. That may make you feel guilty, and it may make the ones you leave feel resentful and angry. Those experienced in moving know and come to rejoice in the reassuring fact that personal networks dissolve and are rejoined with amazing rapidity and solidity. But moving means dislocation and the disruption of one established network of relations and the beginning of a new one in a new place. The pattern is multiplied by the number of persons involved in a family making the move, and some members of the family are better and some are worse at making and breaking the network.

A third meaning of *moving* is very positive, so positive that in fact it may be what makes us preserve the nomadic tradition. Moving means new possibilities. While moving means dislocation and disruption, it also means the chance to reorder for the better. Of course, *better* is an imprecise term. What unfolds eventually may or may not be better according to one's own definition of the term. But moving is clearly the possibility that preferred changes can be made. One's work and the many compensations it brings may be better. The whole core of family needs and opportunities may be better. Even your own essential self may change for the better. Therefore, moving means that all things may be bright and beautiful.

It is the lure of that prospect that makes us first inquisitive and then hopeful about new locations and new networks. That is good. It is also possible that the lure of what might be obscures the perception of what is in the new reality. The height of one's expectations when one moves sets the limits on the melancholy that is sure to follow when the move is accomplished. Nothing measures up to our highest expectations; we never move to Eden. But the power of new possibilities is both valid and vital. To move is to begin afresh. The purpose of this book is to help make those proper expectations lively and creative elements in your thinking and planning.

What It Means for a Minister to Move

Those three meanings of *moving* are universal; clergy are not exceptions. But these words are directed to a particular subgroup: pastors of local churches. It is, therefore, necessary to name some of the special elements in the experience of moving as they pertain to that group.

Clergy moves involve a wide spectrum of concerns and interests. Most clergy live where they work. Town and church become twin focuses in the decision to move. Because of that special aspect of ministerial moves much has to be considered: the school system for children; the type of community where the church is; the types of persons who live there; the social, political, economic structure of the town; and often a parsonage, or manse, is part of the spectrum of considerations. Most people move to change jobs, and then decide where to live so they can do their work; with clergy the choice is one.

Incidentally, this anomaly about the ministerial profession says much about the dissatisfaction many clergy have about the so-called placement system. It is one thing to match the right clergy to the right church; it is something else to match the right family with the right community. The placement system, or lack thereof, seems cumbersome because it has to do more than the system is capable of doing.

Another implication of this professional anomaly is that there is so much more to look for when one is considering a move. It also means that clergy move from place to place with a wide-ranging variety of motives and needs. And it means that those expectations of new possibilities range far and wide.

Another element in what it means for clergy to move is a strong sense of "religion in vocation." Clergy become clergy because of a high religious consciousness. Whatever qualifications they bring to the call, clergy believe that God has called them to their vocation. It follows that clergy moves involve personal religious questions: Am I called of God to minister in Christ's name in this place? Am I doing the will of God for me in making this move? What gifts of the Spirit have I been given that can be shared with these people? Are my prayers for guidance answered in the decision to move, or is my sinful self-interest obscuring contrary messages?

Finally, unique in clergy moves are concerns for career patterns. This is a relatively new element in clergy moving patterns; or at least systematic depiction and discussion of such patterns is new. It is only in the last decade that career counseling centers for clergy have come into existence. Perhaps because the conception of ministry as a career is relatively new, there are many confusions for a minister about his own career and his personal responsibility for its development.

Unlike corporate career models, salary for clergy is not a distinguishing factor. The top and the bottom are not widely separated. Pastors of local churches have tended to substitute size of congregation as the measure of what is top and bottom. In short, bigger is better. The conventional wisdom on the subject has been that one always moves to a bigger church. Fortunately, there are signs that the conventional wisdom is beginning to crumble. First, there is a growing recognition that most churches in America are small. And what is even more hopeful, there is a growing recognition that the small church has certain desirable characteristics, viz., many are ideal for intimate interpersonal relationships. Clergy demographics are important factors in this slowly changing attitude toward the small church. Also involved is the highly publicized clergy surplus. In truth, there are more churches than there are clergy. But also in truth, many churches are said to be not "economically viable." (Translation: They cannot afford full-time clergy.) So, there is no clergy surplus at the first- or even second-level placement, but there is as the career pattern of bigger and better takes hold. There are more clergy desiring appointment to middle and large churches than there are churches for them, and as long as this pattern holds true there will be a clergy surplus.

The laws of supply and demand are producing some inexorable and some painful changes. The emergence of the so-called tentmaker ministry is one aspect of this demographic realignment. These changes also have their cruel side: Older ministers and female ministers feel the crunch on later appointment.

The crumbling conventional wisdom that bigger is better is forcing reexamination where reexamination ought to take place—in clergy's career expectations. Data cannot be marshaled to prove the point, but an informed hunch has it that many clergy want to move because they think their career pattern requires them to do so. It is true that clergy have an "itinerant tradition." Circuit riders suited the American frontier. Clergy develop their own "in" language. One clergy says to another: "I have been here about five years; I have done all I can do here." The other clergy nod their heads sagaciously. They know what that means. Dr. James Glasse of Lancaster Theological Seminary puts the question through his "Clergy Language

Translator." He wants to know: "Does a doctor say, 'I have been here five years; I have healed about all the sick I can here'? Does a lawyer say, 'I have been here about five years; I have won about all the cases I can win here'? Why, then, when clergy use that language, do others nod their heads in sagacious understanding?"

It is because clergy accept a presupposition about career patterns. It is good to reexamine those suppositions. Again, no hard data exist to prove the point, but an informed hunch is that our frequent moves cost the whole church millions of dollars annually. The cost is not in moving expenses. The cost is in trust-building and congregation development, which take a long time and are disrupted by the frequent moves of church leadership.

There are no simple advocacies about how a new career pattern might be designed for clergy. But it is desirable that the reformation begin. It should begin with clergy reading this book as they contemplate or execute a new pastorate. My own advocacy is that the proper place to begin is with job satisfaction and enrichment. That begins in a new pastorate. And that is why the way you begin it is so important. How you begin sets a pattern for finding that job enrichment and job satisfaction that are among the new possibilities moving entails: This time you *may* stay a lifetime.

Your Professional Keys
Despite what the internal monologue preceding this chapter said about the key case that empties and

symbolizes the coming and going of the moment, you are not deprived of all your keys. You have some in your person and in your profession. These keys are the ones to keep and use throughout the whole moving process. They will open and secure many a door through which you must pass. These keys represent the skills, resources, and techniques applicable to ministry in general and to the process of beginning a new pastorate in particular.

Intentionality

Intentionality is one of the buzz words of contemporary conceptions of ministry. Its frequent and flippant use diminishes its creative power. That is too bad, for the word has enormous personal and professional potential.

Intentionality in ministry, simply put, means not responding viscerally and instinctively to every experience. Stated positively, intentionality means having a well-designed, purposive plan that names desired accomplishments, the means to reach them, and, most important, the desire to do so. Rigidity and intentionality are not the same things. Too much that is good in ministry is spontaneous and innovative to insist upon inflexible designs. On the other hand, too much of what happens in ministry is without design and purpose. Personal freedom about shaping one's work is characteristic of the ministerial vocation, as tradition in the execution of that work is also characteristic. The existence of freedom and tradition to such a large degree is both good and bad. It is bad

27

when one does simply what one pleases, or when one does what one has always done. It is good when one acknowledges the presence and gifts of freedom *and* tradition in what one does and willfully attempts to maximize, preserve, and extend those givens.

Intentionality in moving is simple to state and very hard to do. It means defining what you want to accomplish by making this move, the design for doing so, and the pursuit of the technique that will result in accomplishment. Personal freedom and tradition will be very strong forces in this move you are considering. They will dominate how you do it, if you let them. Without intentionality you will move responding to every instance as the particular instance seems to require, and/or you will make this move in essentially the same pattern you have made every previous move in your life. It will be as if you have learned absolutely nothing in the process. And it will be likely that you will learn absolutely nothing in the new process. You might as well have stayed where you were.

Negotiation

The second key you have is concomitant with intentionality. *Negotiation,* too, is a buzz word of contemporary concepts of ministry. It too suffers from frequent use and abuse. The term suffers from sinister, secular implications. It sounds like labor and management belting out an agreement in a smoke-filled brawl room. Clergy, rightly so, want no part of heavy-handed pressure, bluffing, and fist-pounding threats. Perish the thought!

Clergy might be more open to the term and the concept, and its execution, if they understood its dynamics in terms of covenant relationships. A covenant requires two parties. Before the covenant is made the parties specify their mutual duties and contributions. (You may have some vague recollection of the wedding ceremony.) Freedom and tradition are presupposed in negotiation. As with intentionality, this is a third element which seeks to maximize both.

In the dynamics of moving, negotiation has both a narrow, specific sense and a broader, more comprehensive sense. In its specific sense *negotiation* refers to the process by which terms of the call are agreed upon. In the larger sense it refers to the process in which who you are and who the congregation is become clearer and more intricately related. In the larger sense, negotiation does not have a terminus; it never finishes; it goes on and on. As it goes on and on, renegotiation takes place. In this larger sense, a terminus must not occur. If it does, the whole covenantal relationship comes apart.

These two keys, intentionality and negotiation, blend into one key which becomes the style of beginning a pastorate. It can be expressed thus: I want to begin this pastoral relationship in such a way that both of us may grow with the passage of time. That simple statement sets in motion a whole series of inquiries, understandings, agreements, and plans that will facilitate and deepen that purpose.

II.

Glasses: How to Look at a Potential Pastorate

This chapter contains thoughts about what a candidate might look for when he visits a prospective pastorate and what a pastoral search committee might look for in interviewing a candidate. Early in the selection process a candidate is invited to visit the church and community. The following vignette is what a minister and his wife might say to each other in their motel room after one day's interview and before he preaches the next morning.

In a Motel Room

"I really hate this," said Margie.

"Gee, I thought there were some very nice parts of town," I said.

"I didn't mean the town," she said, kicking off her shoes. "I meant this—this interviewing process. Honestly, I feel like an animal in the zoo. Did you see the way that Mrs. Dalton kept looking at me? She knows where every item in my whole wardrobe came from and how much I paid for each part. No, sir, I don't like this. Let's go home."

"Honey," I said, "we can't go home. I have to preach tomorrow. We told them we would visit with them for two days. Now, what do you think of the church?"

"I like the church very much, but—." Margie always has a "but" that makes two different sentences. "But it was very dirty. Did you say they have a *full-time* custodian?"

"I didn't notice it was dirty," I responded. "I like the contemporary lines of the sanctuary, and I could see myself standing in that pulpit."

"Each child would have his own room," she said.

"In the church?" I asked.

"No, Bob, pay attention to what I'm saying; don't go off thinking by yourself. In the parsonage there were four bedrooms. Did you notice that?"

"Oh, yeah, I noticed, but I also noticed that it was on a corner lot. That means about twice as much snow as I am used to shoveling.

"I wonder why that Sam Bird guy asked me if I believe in the Virgin Birth. I haven't been asked that since I left seminary. I wonder if this is a conservative congregation. You know what I wish I had said to him? Boy, if he brings it up again tomorrow, will I be ready for him! I should have said, 'Well, Mr. Bird, I believe exactly what Paul said about the Virgin Birth.' That would have fixed him. I wish I had thought quick enough to say that. I wonder why he asked that question. It's all right to ask those questions, but I wonder what he meant by it."

"The high school would be smaller for Eddie," she said. "I bet he would have a chance to be involved in a lot more things."

"Yeah," I said, "but would it prepare him for a good college? Colleges are awfully selective these days. What high school you come from could make a big difference in the college you go to, and the college you go to could make a big difference in the grad school you go to, and that could make a big difference—"

"Bob, come back to New Town," demanded Margie. "We're supposed to be looking at this town, not settling the whole future."

"Yeah, I know," I said. "But at my age this church may be my whole future. You have to think of that. I don't see much potential for growth around here."

"Neither do I," she said. "But there seemed to be about one of everything you need here."

"One what?"

"One of every kind of store, silly, didn't you notice?"

"No, I guess I didn't notice that," I confessed.

"I wonder, though," she went on, "whether they would have an opening for a dietician in this town. You know, I should work when the kids are in college."

"Now who's jumping into the future? Besides, you may not have to work if I take this job," I said smiling.

"What's the salary?" she asked, straight-faced.

I stopped smiling. "That's something I must remember to ask them tomorrow. Let's try to get some sleep. I want to be at my best tomorrow."

"Bob?"

"Yes?"

"What did Paul say about the Virgin Birth?"

Differing polities means that the interview between prospective pastor and newly vacated church takes place in differing circumstances. Almost always there is some kind of first meeting before the parties make a decision about each other. A sad fact about the moving process is that two parties make a decision consequential to each on the barest amount of data. You may know more about the used car you buy than the church to which you are called. The key to intentionality is to begin work here, in the very early stages of a pastoral relationship. At this point in the process, intentionality is finding out as much as you possibly can about the recently vacated church and all that goes with a move to that place. In addition, intentionality in this early stage means to disclose as much of your true self as you can so that the pastoral search committee can get a true and clear picture of who you are and what you can and cannot do. If your primary intention is to seek a relationship of mutual growth, then now is the time. And the technique is mutual candor.

Some clergy and some search committees play games with each other. They say to each what they think the other wants to hear. They ignore what ought not be ignored. The potential of rejection is present any time two parties are establishing a loving relationship. (Remember the first time you were jilted? It hurts, and no one wants to be rejected through his own inadequacies. But a bad marriage lasts longer than a heart broken by rejection.)

The objective of the placement system by whatever polity is to match the right person with the right church. There is a near-infinite variety of churches and of persons. The chances for error are great, but the chances are markedly reduced by intentionality. The title of this chapter is "Glasses." Glasses are instruments designed to help one see clearly. You see with your brain, but the brain needs as clear and sharp a picture of reality as possible. In this case, glasses bring that clarity and sharpness by correcting different visual imperceptions.

The Minister's Glasses

Begin with yourself. What are you really looking for? How realistic are your expectations? Why do you want to make this move?

The placement system, it was suggested earlier, is a source of discontent because it has too much to do. Another complaint is that too few persons are involved in it. The number may be as small as the minister and the district superintendent. Together you reach a decision of great importance, but would it not be better to have more diverse input on that decision? As ministry is a shared vocation, would it not be better to have a wider sharing in the placement system?

A very important part of what you see through your glasses when you look at a new pastorate can be supplied by the vision of others. Let a trusted colleague hear you speak out loud about the motivations of your move. Ask him not to offer his opinions but rather to help you clarify your thinking.

Family patterns are important too. If your family is open and candid about other things, then the subject of the family's decision to move may be the proper one to discuss with them. See what they all see through their respective glasses. As a rule, kids are more conservative than grown-ups on the subject of moving. But if you subsequently decide to move, it will help you to know in advance what the children will be most concerned about giving up.

The career counseling centers mentioned earlier can be helpful in objectifying what you may or may not know intuitively about yourself. It might be a good idea to take their vocational tests. At least they give some objective data that you can talk over with an objective third party not directly involved in the placement system.

But most important, you are the best font of information about why you want to move and what you need in a new position. The reason for talking it over with others is that it is very hard to talk truthfully with yourself about these matters. Generally speaking, if your own reasons for moving consist in dissatisfaction with the place you are in, then it is likely—not definite, just likely—that you will take those dissatisfactions with you when you move.

On the positive side, Jim Glasse has a generalization that may be helpful in discerning your own motives. He says that clergy are overworked and underemployed. By that I think he means that there are specialties even within the general practice of ministry. Satisfaction in employment results from matching your best skill with a church that most needs that skill. This rule of thumb is not foolproof, of course, because no church requires a single skill; like bananas, skills come in bunches.

Whatever your method, the first step toward a pastorate of mutual growth is your best assessment of who you are, what you have to offer, what you need, and why you want to move. Your assessment is never precise, but the fuzzier it is to you, the fuzzier will be your picture of a new pastorate.

Documentation

Intentionality in looking at a recently vacant church requires homework. When you begin to look at a particular church, not just thinking about moving, you need to be as particular as you can be. *Never* go to an interview without first investigating. If you have neither the time nor the will to do that, you might as well abandon any notion of intentionality.

Before you meet with the pastoral search committee you should request documentation about the church.

Some denominations require a church profile similar to the profile the pastoral search committee will have from you. Whether or not that is available you should also request a constitution, the last annual report, and a history of the church, including the length of recent pastorates. You must read these with your critical glasses. What does the constitution say about the minister's duties? (They are almost always understated.) What can you learn about the church's program and finances from the annual reports? Church histories are almost always revisionist, i.e., they find in the past what seems important to mention from the perspective of the moment. Furthermore, church histories usually follow an outline built around either real estate or pastorates and rarely around ministry or outreach. They usually tell little about the flavor of the congregation.

There is additional information you can gather about the church. This is not exactly documentation because much of it is hearsay and should be treated accordingly. A judicatory official should know something about the recent history and performance of the church. In addition, other clergy are sources of information about particular churches. While the chitchat at convention after-hours sessions is usually of the grapevine nature, it can sometimes produce questions that are worth following up on in an interview. If you know a minister of another denomination in the town where the church is located, that person is a very special resource to you. He knows both town and church very well.

Your homework should also include assembling documentation about the town or area in which the church is located, as you will live where you work. It is easier to learn about towns or areas than about particular churches.

If you can arrange it, a drive to the community in advance of the interview enables you to look at what you want to see. If you cannot do that, your public library may have statistical data on the social and economic composition of the community. Send for several back issues of the local paper. Read the news and the ads. Real estate ads can be revealing if you want to own your own home.

All this data is worth considering. Remember that it is fragmentary, impressionistic, and highly unreliable. Nevertheless, it may pose some questions for further exploration.

A Note to the Pastoral Search Committee
The pastoral search committee too have their glasses. They need also to begin looking at themselves: What are the strengths and weaknesses of our church? What kind of leadership do we most need just now? What is the special mission of our church in our particular community?

One of the obvious differences between you as a pastoral search committee and the pastor you will interview is that you are plural and he is singular. Long before you talk to any minister, you must spend hours together so that your picture of what your church is and might become is cohesive and not a collage of differing pictures. You have been chosen so that collectively you represent the larger congregation.

You, too, have homework to do. There are official channels for the flow of information. They were established to help you secure the information you need. You move outside those channels at your own peril. You are not the first pastoral search committee that was ever created. You are well advised to follow the customs and procedures that your denomination has established over the years. They are certainly not foolproof, but they are more reliable than a Ouija board approach.

You have every right to expect your denominational channels to provide you with some documentation on potential ministers. Most ministers have a dossier or profile that should be made available. Usually, references are given on that profile. Since the Buckley Amendment has made confidential information very hard to come by, you are within your rights to converse personally with those references. Ministerial credentials are kept on file. You can find out where the person went to school and what his or her previous work record has been. Printed material by or about the minister may also be available.

You should comply with all requests clergy make of you about your church and community. If you really want to capture their attention, you should prepare in advance a packet of information about your church and community. Send them all the relevant information and pictures. This is an opportunity for you to put your best foot forward.

The Interview

Having done as much advance data-gathering as possible, there comes a time when you actually want to meet the potential candidate.

The session need not be an inquisition to either party. Your mutual intention is to get acquainted. You both know why you are together, and you need not play coy games about your purpose.

It helps to have a congenial atmosphere. You should make the candidate and his wife comfortable in public accommodations. A dinner or social gathering usually helps relax the mood.

Candor is catching. A format that you may want to consider involves a measure of storytelling. Some members of the committee may want to share how they came to be associated with the church and what it has come to mean to them over the years. The candidate may want to tell of his pilgrimage in the ministry, mentioning some of the people and places that have been significant to him.

You may then want to turn to the specifics of your past ministries: "Our church needs to grow in the areas of—." "I have been thinking that I should be where—."

There should be an opportunity to correct misinformation or raise questions that the data-gathering has produced. If irregularities have emerged—a checkered career pattern on the part of the candidate, a succession of short pastorates at the church—these should be faced and discussed in the first interview.

Sometimes, but not always, the candidate preaches a sermon, but never in the pulpit of the church he is considering. If that is not possible, a tape recording of a sermon from back home will have to do. After the sermon a second interview is sometimes held, not to evaluate the sermon but to continue the conversation begun with areas of mutual interest not yet covered.

The interview should conclude not with a decision but with a promise on both parts. The chairperson of the search committee should say to the minister, "We will be in touch with you again in X number of weeks." (The message may be that we have decided not to pursue our conversation further, but that need not be said on the spot.) Similarly, the minister should say that he will continue to think about this conversation further. (He may decide not to think positively about the conversation, but he need not say that at this time.) What is important is that both parties understand that communication about next steps will take place in a fixed period of time.

It's All Right to Say "No, Thanks"

Usually, the initiative after the first interview is with the committee. They have pledged to keep the candidate informed about next steps. After that communique the initiative is with the candidate. He must encourage or discourage the committee from further talk. No one is obligated beyond that first interview. Neither party owes the other anything except the courtesy of a prompt reply.

It is very hard to say no. The committee hates to say no to anyone, especially to a minister. Ministers are notoriously bad about saying no. They get into more mischief by their strong desire to please. But if reservations on either part emerge, a lack of enthusiasm, or a clear dislike, the proper and timely act is to say no right then and there. An explanation is unnecessary; just make the response definite. There is no need to play hard to get or to ask for the moon as a condition of reopening conversations. Just cut it at this point.

Cut it and assume that the system is working. Working? How can you say that when I did not get the job? How can you say that when we did not get the person we had finally agreed on?

Nevertheless, the system has worked. Its purpose is to match the right person with the right church. That takes two compatible components. If only one part is willing, then the whole will not work. In the opening vignette it was said that the system was hated. That may be true, but it is preferable to the alternative of putting names into a hat and pulling out the first name when a vacancy occurs. In that procedure both freedom and tradition lose. But when the system is applied with intention, freedom and tradition make for good choices. It starts two parties on the way to a pastoral relationship in which both parties continue to grow.

III

Coins: Making Decisions

An Exchange of Letters

Dear Mr. Kemper:

This letter comes to inform you that our committee has met subsequent to your visit with us, and we have decided to invite you to have substantive conversations with us about our pastoral vacancy. We have decided to suspend all other conversations with other candidates.

We hope you will find it possible to return to our community within the next two weeks. Some of the members of our committee feel that we do not know enough about your views on some matters critical to our church. We also hope that your visit might give us an opportunity to begin talking about the terms of a call.

By this letter we want you to know that we are very

43

interested in you and in continuing conversations with you. At the same time, we are not in a position to recommend you to the congregation until we have resolved some unanswered questions. We are hopeful you will accept our invitation to return for further discussions. We look forward to meeting with you soon.

Sincerely yours,
William T. Reace, Chairperson
Pastoral Search Committee
New Town Church

Dear Mr. Reace:

Thank you for your letter inviting me to return to New Town for further conversations with your committee. I understand that this is not a call but that you are interested in serious conversations about the leadership of your church and the terms of call. I further understand that neither of us is contractually obligated at this point.

Having given thoughtful and prayerful consideration to your invitation, I am pleased to inform you that I would welcome the opportunity for further discussions with your committee. I will plan to meet with the committee one week from tomorrow if that is agreeable with you.

I am eager to talk with you about our mutual future. I have some ideas I would like to share with the committee about the kind of ministry we might have together in New Town.

Yours truly,
Robert G. Kemper

It is decision-making time. It is a great time; it is an agonizing time. You have gathered as much data about the church and community as possible. You have met the committee for the first time, and they are interested in you. Now what?

This chapter is entitled "Coins." The title is meant to suggest what decision-making does to you. Two sides of a decision wage war in your mind, and in desperation you find yourself thinking, "Heads I stay, tails I go." That is not intentional decision-making. The freedom to say yes or no is what makes decision-making so vexing. Intentional decision-making is a way of reducing the vacillation freedom provokes.

Understanding the Moment

Intentional decision-making is an attempt to understand and conduct decision-making in stages with spaces in between the stages. It treats decision-making not as the flipping of a coin but as a process. The technique required is isolating the separate parts and dealing with each one in particular while understanding that each is part of a total process that will arrive at a conclusion.

It is very important to provide some space in the process. The exchange of letters cited at the beginning of this chapter illustrates the spacing process. The committee is interested in the candidate; the candidate is interested in the church. That is stage one: an expression of mutual interest in further explorations. Neither party has made a commitment beyond that of

45

increasing interest. It may be that the committee is not yet unanimous in its selection of you. It is desirable that they be so, and the extra time may help the uncommitted know their minds. Also, you may be favorably inclined, but there are some gaps of information about the church and its expectations that you need to explore with them. Furthermore, you need some space to prepare for the negotiations about the terms of the call. Stage two: Put in motion the specifics of your larger intention about mutual growth. The third stage will be the development of the terms of call. That is where the specifics of your relationship to the church will be made. The fourth and final stage is agreement on the terms and the beginning of a new pastorate.

It is important throughout these steps that both parties have the right to say no. If they say no, it may mean the end of the process, or it may mean that the process will have to take another direction. But without the right to say no, railroading may be apparent to either party, and the final process will not result in a mutual, cooperative agreement.

What Decision-Making Does to You

Decision-making affects you. You should anticipate its effects and not panic when they come upon you. You are unique, and how you respond to crisis (in the sense of critical moments in which a future is affected) will be unique to your personality. But it is highly likely that some of the following experiences will be yours.

The decision will be preeminent in your life. It will dominate who you are, what you do, what you say. It will be very difficult to continue your work in your present position. You may feel guilty, guilty about the current duplicity and guilty about leaving. You may have a high desire to talk a lot. Your private thoughts need to be voiced. But to whom? It is better to talk to your wife and family than to the chairperson of the official board at this point. And, you are likely to be plagued by ambiguity; the two sides of the coin will keep turning over in your mind.

Prayer is helpful in the decision-making process. Not prayers that plead for signs, but prayers that raise your consciousness to the awareness of mission, commitment, care for others, and the servant role you have pledged in ordination. Personal faith is not extraneous to these decisions; it is the means by which you make the decisions. Intentionality is not a tool you bring in for this purpose only. It is one of the elements in your faith. Willfully directing your thoughts back to the basics in prayer and meditation does not produce specific answers, but it definitely sharpens the questions: Who am I? To whom do I owe my loyalties? What is the purpose of my creation? What is the good life for me? All are relevant, provocative questions that make the decision before you an example or a footnote to the larger questions. They form the backdrop to the particular decision before you. A genuine sense of call emerges not from the particularities of a specific church you are considering but from the generalities of what you believe about yourself and your relation to God, Christ, and the church.

Planning to Plan

Part of the vexation of intentional decision-making is that it often requires bi-level and even tri-level thinking. As the stages of the decision unfold, you must deal intensely with each one, but at the same time you must be thinking of the future. Before the second interview (if there is one) and certainly before the terms of call are agreed to, you need to do some intentional planning about beginning the new pastorate.

Peter Drucker, well-known writer on management, remarks that when he is called to a company for consultation, his first question is always, What are you trying to accomplish? The basic point is that you organize in order to meet your goals, whatever it is you seek to accomplish. Form follows function.

What is suggested here is that this decision-making stage, like a coin, has two faces. One concerns whether to become pastor of the new church. The other, equally important, pertains to what kind of ministry to have in the new church. In the long term the second question is more important than the first. Whether you are fully aware of it or not, the answer to what kind of ministry to have is being shaped even before you have fully decided to be the minister.

Thus, in the muddle of decision-making about the position, you must have a bi-level focus on the kind of ministry you want to have. Even without knowing the people in the new congregation there are some elements that you can plan intentionally to accomplish right now.

First, you can plan right now to build trust. All religious institutions are voluntary organizations. They are held together by trust, mutual trust among the members and between the members and the minister. High in your planning is the development of a trust relationship between this congregation and yourself. It has already begun with the pastoral search committee, and the committee has a role to play in furthering it with the congregation.

Second, you can plan to deal with grief. To be sure, there is a rising tide of festive celebration in the decision-making process, but there is also an undertow of grief in that tide. The church is in a grieving process: You will be losing a church; the church its minister. Your family will be grieving for all the associations they have had. Now is the time to allow some space in your life and in the life of that congregation for the grieving process to run its course.

Third, you need to plan now to be the teacher of the congregation. They do not know who you are; so you will have to teach them about yourself. They know something about ministers, but what they know is very diverse and probably inaccurate. You need to teach them about the ministry in general as well as about yourself in particular. That teaching process has already begun. Needed now is an intentional plan for teaching this particular congregation about the ministry. How do you want to be seen by this

49

congregation? If as open and warm, then you need to think of ways that from the very beginning allow you to be understood as being open and warm. What about your personal life-style? Are you a workaholic? Do you pace yourself? The way you begin is likely to be the way in which you will continue. Now is the beginning.

Planning to Leave

The Roman god Janus (after whom the month of January is named) is depicted with two faces: one looking forward, one looking backward. You have come to a "Janus moment." One part of you looks forward with intention toward what is yet to be; another part of you looks with intention to the dissolution of what has been. It is awkward and ambiguous but a necessary part of the process.

A tri-level focus for this moment is the anticipation of your departure. It may not happen, but if it does you need to be intentional about it. At a procedural level you need to know what custom or contract requires of you in terms of resignation: To whom? Within what time frame?

At some point the lay leadership of your congregation needs to be told of developments. It is hard to say just when. The parameters are clear. Say nothing until you have reached a firm understanding with the new church, and say something before it reaches your lay leaders by rumor or gossip.

But more than procedure, you owe it to your present congregation to leave them with intention. Be intentional about the process to be followed in the interim, the process for a successor, and above all, the process for facilitating grief.

As you reach a decision about the new church you will experience a change in yourself: You become future-oriented. You can become so absorbed in the future that you neglect the present and forget the past. That is regrettable for both you and your present congregation. You both need to name the moments that have been significant to you. You need to share the data about the congregation that you have accumulated in your tenure as pastor. But most important, you need to say farewell. You need to say it from the pulpit, to persons and groups, socially, pastorally, and to yourself.

Somehow, in the depiction of these stages of decision-making, in the multilevel aspects of decision, and in the anticipation of grief, this process sounds heavy, laborious, and vexing. That is not the truth. On the contrary, it shakes you from the lethargy of routine, the boredom of the usual. It is very exciting. It is highly stimulating. You come awake and alive. It feels good.

If all you did was flip a coin and decide on what comes up, the old routines would go on. You would go from one place to another. The church you leave would survive. The church to which you are going would welcome you. So, what's the sweat? There is no sweat. It is intentional ministry that makes the difference. It is quite possible just to do what you want to do and to hang loose about everything else. But for those who want to savor the moment, who want their ministry to have purpose and direction, who want to use tools to fulfill their responsibilities and keep their vows, who want to learn from their past that they may grow in their future, intentional decision-making is not a burden. It is a means to some highly desirable ends.

IV.

Plan A: Before You Go to a New Pastorate

The End of a Negotiating Session

"I must say, Bob, this has been an eye-opening experience for me," said Bill Reace as he leaned back in his chair. "I never knew there was so much involved in being a minister. To tell you the truth, I didn't expect this. I thought once we decided on you, and I related what we had done for Ken before you, we would just agree on that. I guess we will have to get used to that. You are not Ken Seim; you are Bob Kemper. Your needs are different from his; your style is different from his.

"In my business I have interviewed and hired a lot of people, but I don't think any of them has known what they wanted as you do. You have given this a lot of thought. I can tell that, and I am glad you have. It helps us. On the other hand, I have to level with you: Some of the things you want will not be understood by this congregation. Your proposals are too new, too different for us. Maybe we will get used to them with the passage of time, at least I know we can get them on the agenda of the official board for future discussion. I understand why you want them, and maybe someday we will be able to get together on them.

"You taught me a lot of things I should have known, but I guess I just didn't pay much attention. For instance, I never thought about you guys always working on Sundays. I thought you just knew you did that; it never occurred to me to think of trading other days for those Sundays you work. I think that is something we need to talk about with the official board. I mean, it really isn't fair to your kids for you to be tied down every single weekend.

"Boy, am I glad this job is about over! All I have to do is get these things in writing for you and the congregation. Honestly, if I had known this was going to take so long and how many meetings I'd have to go to, I would never have agreed to be chairman. But I think we did a good job. Sometime later I'll tell you some of the funny situations we got into—like when we tried to visit your church inconspicuously and were made to stand up during the service and tell where we were from. Oh, brother!

"What's that you say, I'm not quite finished? What more do we have to do? You surely cannot have any more items to negotiate! Oh, you mean getting ready for the transition—all those things I need to do with the board and committees of the church and the whole congregation. I didn't forget what you said about the importance of interpreting these things to the congregation. You can count on that. What I meant is that doing that is not work; that's going to be fun. I need some fun after these months. I think we are going to have a terrific time together. Let's get going."

A decision has been made, but the process is not completed. Indeed, the intentional beginning of a new pastorate is about to unfold. They have decided to recommend you, and only you, to the congregation to be their new pastor. You have agreed that if the congregation extends the formal call to you, you will accept it.

Sometime between the decision to be the new pastor and the issuance of the call, there is a crucial stage. It is the development of the terms of call, the specification of what will constitute the relationship between the two parties. The arrival at those terms of call is sometimes called "the negotiation" (using the term in its narrow sense). This is often done between the pastor and the chairperson of the search committee. It is best to have few, but influential, people involved.

Understanding Negotiations

The decision to be pastor of this church is behind you. The question before you is the *kind* of pastorate you want to establish together. If your intention is to establish a long-lasting relationship that provides for mutual growth, there are some designs that ought to be negotiated.

The minister should be aggressive in negotiation. He should be prepared to state his desired terms. He must also be prepared to compromise. Not all the elements he desires may be specified, or even acceptable, for further discussion. This chapter is called "Plan A." It suggests specific items you may want to include in the negotiations about the terms of call. These terms are unlikely to receive much attention after you have been there several years. But timing is important, and the time for Plan A is before you begin, not afterward. Therefore, have your terms ready when the time comes to negotiate.

Plan B will be set forth in a subsequent chapter. It is not an alternative but an extension of the intentional principle. Plan B will specify intentional goals for beginning a new pastorate.

Tradition, you should know, will be a powerful element in the process. The church to which you are going may or may not have had a long and mutually rewarding relationship with your predecessor; but the point is that they are not without experience when it comes to relating to ministers. They will want very much to fit you into the mold with which they are most comfortable. If you are comfortable, say no contrary word; the terms will be decided by tradition. That may be fine: Tradition usually lasts because it works.

Further, many clergy are reluctant to be aggressive in negotiation. It simply is not in them to ask for anything, just accept what is offered. That is fine, too, provided they have a concomitant quality: to be happy with what they get. That is both possible and desirable. What is impossible and not desirable are the clergy types who withhold their designs from the negotiating process, and then complain about the shabby treatment of churches toward clergy. You cannot have it two ways. Make your peace with your own style.

The negotiating process should arrive at some conclusions. It is highly desirable to put into writing what has been agreed. These may or may not be the specific terms of call. It may be preferable for the terms of call to be general and purposely vague. But if that is the case, there should be a separate letter in your files from the chairperson of the search committee that specifically itemizes what was agreed to. Some people may think it a violation of trust to require this in writing, but on the other hand documentation was helpful in researching a pastorate, and documentation may be helpful in developing a pastoral relationship. Writing it out objectifies it for all to see. The best reason for writing it out is that church leadership changes. It is possible that within three years you will be dealing with an entirely different set of lay leaders. It may not be a bad idea to have each succeeding lay leader read what was agreed to by their predecessors.

Once the specifics are agreed to, it is the duty of the pastoral search committee to transmit these to the appropriate boards and committees. Whether they need to be made known to the whole congregation depends in part on the polity you follow. Generally, only the lay leadership need to know the specifics. But, especially if there are substantive changes from the past, the pastoral search committee must communicate those changes to the existing boards and committees. You need to understand that sometimes they cannot agree to what has been proposed.

What if a snag develops? Maybe you and the chairperson cannot reach an understanding. Maybe the chairperson cannot get a lay committee to agree. What do you do then? You calculate. You calculate how important the item is to the general intention of a lasting pastorate. If you believe it is essential, then you can withdraw from the negotiations. That is to be avoided and done only in extreme circumstances. It embarrasses everyone. A far more likely stance is to accept a compromise. Agree to continue to work on the particular item. Make sure it gets on the right agenda, and keep it there until it is resolved. The third alternative is to forget it. Just back off, saying, in effect, that it is not an essential item: We will drop it from further consideration.

Here is a generalization to keep in mind: In the unfolding placement and decision, the needs of the church usually dominate. The church is in a more advantageous position in that it can define its needs and look at persons from the standpoint of those needs. They have narrowed the choice to you. They think you are the one for them. Then the balance shifts. Now the minister says, "If I am the one for you, then here is what I think I need in order to do the best job for you." That generalization is made not to encourage power plays but to help clarify the dynamics and to underscore the importance of timing. The wrong agenda at the wrong time can derail satisfactory conversations on either party's part.

When the terms of call are agreed to, the pastoral search committee needs to communicate the terms with the committees, to report to the congregation, and, if your polity requires, secure the congregation's favorable vote. A good pastoral search committee can do still more. They may want personally or collectively to make you feel welcome when you arrive in the new town. (Remember, in the first vignette, how good the new minister felt when the chairman called the night before he left his former home to go to the new one.) But even beyond that, the pastoral search committee may want to gather for a festive occasion to celebrate the good job they did and the good times they had doing their job. If the process has gone on for some time, they may have become an intimate fellowship and may very much want to renew that fellowship from time to time. Furthermore, an informal annual review with the committee during the years of your tenure as minister may be a very good idea. You may get some of your most reliable and candid feedback from such a group. They were chosen in the first place because they were representative of the congregation. Keep in touch with them when you begin and as you develop in the new pastorate.

Meanwhile, Back at the Ranch

When the terms of call have been agreed to, it is time to tell the lay leadership of your present congregation what is about to happen. Your polity may specify who that will be. You should not tell the whole congregation until you have received and accepted the official call. A slip would be embarrassing to you. The lay officers need you to tell them what denominational procedures are for discovering candidates, your wisdom on provisions during the interim, your thoughts on the needs of the church just now, and how you would like to say farewell.

Be prepared for an outpouring of shock and disbelief. Many will feel betrayed and hurt. There are certain euphemisms you will hear, e.g., "I am glad that you had a chance to better yourself," "How will we ever get along without you?" Be assured that the church got along before you, and it will after you. But let their grief and yours be genuine, open, and understood.

Your denominational colleagues need to know what is happening. They may have been party to the negotiations, or they may not have been. If they have not, it is essential that you notify them of your decision to accept the call. That information sets in motion some important record-keeping that needs to be done on your behalf.

Items for Negotiation Before You Accept the Call

What follows here are the specific items of a negotiation. They have been used by the author.

However, they are clearly suggestive and in no way prescriptive. As components of compensation are easier to identify and specify than duties, the following specifics of compensation are disproportionate in their importance. To be sure, items of compensation should be specific; but the attempt to define duties is of greater importance in the future of the pastoral relationship. You will want to develop your own agenda. These may stimulate your own thinking about the kind of ministry you want to have in your new pastorate.

Salary Provisions

Base Salary. Clergy, for a lot of good reasons, are not very sophisticated in economic and financial matters. One of their mistakes is to confuse salary and professional expenses. These need to be separated: One represents compensation for services; the other is meant to reimburse you for the costs of providing the services.

The most important item in the financial provisions is your base salary. That is what you will receive as compensation for being minister of the church. No one, but no one, knows how to arrive at a fair and adequate salary for clergy. It is a fact that clergy are among the lowest compensated professionals. It is also a fact that the vow of poverty has a strong and noble tradition in Christendom. (Poverty ought to be linked with chastity unless the whole family takes the vow.) I am a rigorous advocate of high salaries for clergy for two simple reasons. Low salaries are a deterrent in the recruitment of the best brains and spirits for the profession. (Why not be a good lay member of the church and the director of a scientific laboratory?) Second, low salaries make clergy materialistic. They count every choice in life in terms of dollars. That is materialism. It is my opinion that your new salary should be considerably higher than your previous salary. There is nothing personal in that advocacy; it is strictly professional. If you do not want the money, give it away; but the level of compensation for the whole profession is deplorable, and you ought to do your part in raising it.

The why of clergy salaries is really another matter. In this matter you may want to know what is fair. You may want to check on the cost of living in this particular community. If you are going to live in a high-cost area, you may suffer what the economists call "dollar illusion." You may be beguiled by a much larger salary, only to find that in real dollars you were better off before your increase in grade. One helpful check is to key the minister's salary to a comparable profession in the community. Some think that the principal of a high school has similar educational requirements, community status, and professional responsibility. No one knows that that is right either, but it may be a helpful guide in arriving at a salary.

Salaries are usually stated in annual amounts. In addition, however, your terms of call should specify the frequency of the installments on that annual salary. How will it be paid to you? Weekly? Monthly?

You will want to know that for your own budgeting.

A very important addition to the specification of annual salary and its installments is the phrase *with annual review.* That means this is a starting, not a lifetime, salary. If you have to, you could demand that the salary be reviewed every year; that is not likely or desirable. The expression of the provision in the terms of call is usually sufficient notification that annual review is the expected pattern.

That is the basic statement about salary: annual amount, installment, policy of review. Some clergy (not the author) prefer more specification. They want it stated what is to be done with fees and honoraria; they want a cost-of-living escalator clause. They want it stated if there are bonuses given in a church. They want a definition of *merit increase.* These items seem more specific than need be in the terms of call, but they may be useful to write into a personnel policy that governs all the employees of the church.

The second item in your financial provisions is pension. Most major denominations have a pension program for clergy—sometimes keyed to salary, sometimes not. The formula for computing the pension and the time installments should be specified. There are so many denominational patterns that it is hard to comment on each, but it is important for clergy to know that what goes into that pension is what they will receive upon retirement. The higher the pension payments now, the better your old age will be.

Some clergy, especially older clergy, want a

supplementary pension program. They may want tax-sheltered annuities. These, too, must be specified in the terms of call. Your denominational officials or reputable financial planners can help you understand the vagaries of the law and the benefits you will receive.

Basically, as minister of the church you are paid financial and deferred compensation. It is customary to include the parsonage as part of the base compensation. The case for doing so is convincing: The provision of a house saves the minister a lot of out-of-pocket expenditure which most lay persons have. But in this itemization, housing will be treated as a professional expense. It is my opinion that there is another compelling reason for doing so: Clergy must live in the town where they work. If you have little choice about that, then it is a cost-of-employment item and not a matter of salary.

Cost of Employment. These items are different from salary, present and deferred. You may very well receive money for these items, but the money is reimbursement, not compensation. Most of these, for instance, are either excluded from federal income tax or are deductions on your income tax. You should approach them with the understanding that they are the necessities for doing the work of ministry. *Necessity* is always a loaded word. You need a suit of clothes, but that is not counted as a necessity. You can go a year or two without any continuing education (some clergy, alas, go a lifetime without it). For negotiating purposes, it is good to name your professional expenses and find the ways in which the church will or will not reimburse you for them.

Housing is the most complicated of these cost-of-employment items. Why this is a cost-of-employment item rather than a compensation item was stated above. Wherever you and your church decide to place you, you still need to do a lot of negotiating about your housing. You may be confronted with a choice about which you must make up your mind before negotiating.

The choice is to live in a parsonage, manse, rectory, or other church-owned housing. If that is your choice, there are still specifications that should be mentioned in the terms. Is the house acceptable to you as it is? Does it need remodeling or redecorating? If so, it should be specified what is to be done and who will do it. Generally, the minister's family should have the maximum freedom about the selection of the decor in their home. At the same time, it is the church's property, and the church should bear the costs of improvement.

The assignment of maintenance and upkeep is also important. Usually a board of trustees has this assignment, and an annual review may be necessary here. No homeowner can let property just exist without painting, replacing things, or changing it over the years. Many churches, however, do just that. An annual inspection may keep up consciousness about the implications of church ownership of property.

Other items about the parsonage are sometimes specified. Will the utilities, including telephone, be

65

paid by the church? Will the custodian have any duties at the parsonage? Who handles lawn care, snow removal, and routine maintenance (e.g., light-bulb replacement)?

A second choice you have about housing is owning or renting your own home. This is not the place for an extended discussion of the relative merits of this option. What is essential is that you know your own mind on the options before you. If your choice is to own your own home, that needs to be specified. You will be paid an agreed upon sum of money to buy your own home. That money is excluded from your income. You are also entitled to deduct normal cost-of-housing expenses, i.e., taxes, interest, etc. All that is needed in the terms of call is the specification of the amount and the installment arrangements.

Much more, however, needs to be understood and agreed to. For instance, you need to know something about the relative cost of homes in the area. You need to guess about utility costs, upkeep, and improvement. The church, if it owns a parsonage, may be faced with the question of selling or renting the current parsonage. They may choose to sell, invest the proceeds, and designate that income as your housing allowance. Under the current provisions of the Internal Revenue Service code, an official body of your church must issue a letter specifying the amount of your housing allowance and enter that specification in their minutes.

The choice is very complicated, with no easy answers for you. If you do decide to buy a home as you begin this new pastorate, it greatly ups the tensions and excitement of the new beginning. On the lighter side, you may be amused by the title of Alan King's book *He Who Owns His Own House Deserves It.*

Transportation Allowance. In the work of ministry you go from place to place to perform your service. This should be an expense of your employer. Clergy who think car allowances are income deceive themselves, for the actual cost of owning and operating a car is not borne fully by most churches. The clergy often subsidize this expense out of their own pockets.

Transportation is a more inclusive term than the customary car. You have taxis, trains, or other conveyances to use. Often the figure is expressed as an annual amount. That needs to be specified along with the installment plan. A few churches require clergy to report church mileage on a regular basis. This is a nuisance, but it is more accurate. Still other churches rent cars for their clergy to use. In that case the church, not you, is the leasee of the car, and it handles expenses. If you receive a specified annual amount, you must report that as income on your taxes, and then deduct the actual costs of operation, including a percentage amount for professional use.

Vacations and Paid Holidays. Your new church probably has a fixed policy on vacations and paid holidays, and that policy will be reiterated in the terms of call. Nevertheless, it is a good item to discuss in negotiation because it raises some interesting features of ministerial work. In short, this item is a good one for teaching about the ministry. Let me give you some background.

Ministers work when everyone else is at leisure. Sundays and many holidays are ministers' busiest days. Most clergy work not only the holidays but the same normal pattern of other people as well. Ours is very confining work, and we need to find trade-offs for this confinement. The clergy were among the first of the professions to receive a month's paid vacation. My father had one in 1929. (Has the world changed that much in fifty years?) The long clergy vacation in those days was a trade-off for the confinement of weekends and holidays. Now that multiple week vacations are common, does the month's vacation mean as much? Have we found a more contemporary way of recognizing this special face of ministerial work? Should we think of nine- and ten-month years as teachers do?

It is not likely that you will change the traditional month's paid vacation, but it may be that others will want you to be freer about your regular workday routine or take mini-vacations whenever you can, like after a major religious holiday. The point is that this unusual feature of who you are and what you do will not surface in the laity's minds unless their consciousness is raised in a negotiating session.

Finally, if you have children of school age, do try to take those paid holidays on Mondays when the culture is at leisure. You will enjoy the special occasions with the family.

Continuing Education. Tradition may also dictate the

specifics on continuing education, but this is another item you may want to use as a good teaching device about the nature of ministry. You are not an inexhaustible font of never-ending wisdom. You need to replenish soul and mind as other people do. A certain number of days and a certain budget will enable you to do so. You may be the congregation's teacher, but you also need to be taught. The item communicates that you are a person still striving to grow and improve in your vocation.

Expense Account. Many clergy subsidize their own ministries when they pay out of pocket for items that are required expenditures in their regular and special services. There are special expenses that any Christian person might incur, but there are other expenses that you as a minister incur. You may go to a monthly luncheon with a group in your church; that is a professional expense, and the cost of attending should be reimbursed.

In most terms of call there is a specified annual amount for expenses. These are paid upon presentation of receipts. You need to keep the records on the items for reimbursement. Sometimes, churches just add a monthly amount to your paycheck for expenses. If they do that, you must report it as income to the IRS and then report all the expenditures under your business deductions. There is less bookkeeping for you if you just voucher your expenses. But some item for expenses should be included in the terms of call. The chances are good that the money will be spent anyway; the issue is, Who is responsible for it?

Health and Disability Insurance. A soaring cost-of-employment item for all employers is health insurance. You dare not be without it. Most churches have a group program that covers you with your denominational standing. (That is another good reason to let denominational officials know about your new pastorates.) Usually the terms of call just say that health insurance will be provided. But there are several variations on this that need to be clarified in the terms of call. Sometimes churches expect clergy to pay a portion of their own premiums. Sometimes they expect the minister to pay an additional premium if he elects to cover his family. And sometimes there are options like dental care that need specification. If by this move you are changing your health insurance, make sure you get a statement of the benefits provided by the particular policy. The chances are good that you will need it sometime during your new pastorate.

Sometimes linked with the health insurance is a disability policy. If there is none, find one and have the premiums specified in the terms of call. This is part of being intentional too. There is nothing sadder than a disabled clergyman and a church struggling to honor its commitments to him and his family, while also sustaining an ongoing program in the minister's absence.

Moving Expense. This item is often written in the call, but it needs to be acted upon before the terms are agreed to. It needs to specify what moving expenses will be paid (transportation and lodging for the family en route?) and who will make the arrangements. You should be free to select your own carrier, but some churches are fussy about an unknown making contracts on their behalf. And usually the mover wants to be paid before he unloads. Some arrangement for payment needs to be cleared.

Sabbatical Leave. It has been the custom in academic circles for professional teachers to be given a period for scholarly study unintruded upon by their normal routines. Clergy need a similar provision. As the name implies, sabbatical grants a leave of time after the completion of seven years of employment. Most churches have variations of the time: They may, for instance, begin eligibility after three years of employment, and then grant something like two weeks' paid absence for every year of employment up to a maximum. This item, too, helps reinforce your image as a scholar, a learner.

Sick Leave. If the church has a policy it should be stated in the terms. If it does not have a policy, it should develop one. Common practice is something like ten sick days a year with pay. If the person is sick for more than ten days, it may be extended to thirty days with pay by the action of a lay board. Sicknesses of more than thirty days necessitate a decision by the board on the rate of compensation. This policy should dovetail with the disability policy so there is no loss of income during an extended illness. The only thing worse than negotiating this policy in the terms of call is negotiating it from your sickbed, when no one

71

knows the right and proper thing to do. Have it in writing in advance.

Social Security. There is not much chance your church will want to talk to you about paying your Social Security. There is even some doubt about whether they can. What is important here is that the church understand that under a peculiarity of the Social Security system you are self-employed. You must pay your F.I.C.A. tax in full. Whatever your salary is, you can subtract the Social Security right off the top. You will not have that money to spend. For many clergy their annual Social Security tax has grown to the point where it is larger than their annual pledge to the church. Manfred Holck of *Church and Clergy Finance* urges churches to budget an item that equals the difference between what an employed person pays from his own wages and what a self-employed person pays—in other words, treat you as if you were an employee even though the law says you are self-employed. The principal reason for doing so, he argues, is not the extra money you have to pay tax on but the guarantee of a raise as the Social Security rate rises. (The Social Security tax paid by many pastors tripled between 1968 and 1978! What if it triples again between 1978 and 1988?) Unless your predecessor was very sophisticated in the laws of Social Security, that will be new ground for your church. They need to know that your salary will be diminished by your Social Security tax.

Thus ends a rather lengthy list of cost-of-employment items for you to discuss with the committee.

These kinds of items probably require further negotiation with other church bodies. You may not want to bother with any or all of these. That is your choice. But the net effect of talking about all these is to clarify the special and unusual nature of your work. And that is highly desirable to both you and the church.

Long as this list is, they are not the really important items of the negotiation. The important items follow, having to do with your role as minister of the church and the ways you go about doing it.

Duties of the Minister

The list of minister's duties needs to be written even though it will be hard to do so. Often a simple paragraph from the constitution of the church is cited here. But this is what all the interviewing and decision-making has been about. An effort should be made to preserve the research that went into your selection. The task of formulating these duties rests primarily with the pastoral search committee, but you should have input in what emerges.

Because this is so hard to write, sometimes a few general catchall phrases are used, such as "to provide leadership for regularly scheduled services of worship" or "to teach the Christian faith to all ages," and then an attempt is made to specify some of the special emphases that this church wants to make in the next few years, such as "to lead us in an expanded program of service and outreach" or "to help us enlist new families in our fellowship." These phrases are very important because they form the special task you have been chosen to do and because they form a standard by which subsequent evaluation of your performance can be made.

It is best if the language and the concept behind it has a "we-ness." The duties are not something the minister is going to do all by himself. Rather, the duties are to be done by the whole church, with the minister aiding and offering resources for what is to be done.

Under the duties it is helpful to have a statement about the relationship of the minister to the rest of the church staff. If it is to be done this way, then a phrase like "All other church employees shall be accountable to the minister" is needed. The particular form of accountability does make a difference and that may not be it, but it is important in the job description to clarify who is responsible to whom. If that takes several church council meetings to get clarified, wait it out; you will be glad it was specified one way or another.

Also under "duties" it is important to mention the minister's relationship to the larger denominational and ecumenical church. It disarms those faultfinders who say you do not pay enough attention to them to learn that when you are away from the local parish you are doing your job.

You may want the duties to include specific committee assignments. This is important if the church is large with a lot of committees and you fear you will never keep up with all their meetings. But, regardless of size, it may help to limit or define the administrative role you are to play within the fixed organization of the local church.

Some ministers (not I) want a phrase in their duties about "a free and open pulpit," meaning that when controversial issues are mentioned the detractors can be directed to the small print of the contract. The freedom of the pulpit is axiomatic, but if you want it specified, bring it up now, not when everyone is shouting at one another.

Clergy are relatively comfortable with vague generalities. In the long run that may be a commendable trait. It maximizes our freedom to shape ministerial work in the way we think it ought to be shaped. But a necessary corrective to that professional freedom are the expectations of lay persons within the churches we serve. By encouraging the laity to specify our duties we are being intentional about our service, and by joining them in specifying our mutual duties we are defining our mission. That is good indeed.

Working Conditions. Sometimes the terms of call make some references to the minister's working conditions. Too often these are assumed to be understood: The assumption lasts until it is clear that neither party has in fact understood working conditions at all.

Staff Accountability. The phrase *staff accountability* seems to refer only to large churches with multiple clergy, but that is not so. Every church has a staff, even if it is a one-day-a-week secretary. A source of constant hassle in churches is interstaff conflict. The new minister is a threat to existing staff members because he is unaware of the tradition that accompanies the position and the person who occupies it. Before the minister meets the staff, the church through its official boards should clarify the policy of accountability. These should be reiterated to all staff members. Many different patterns prevail. All staff members are accountable to the minister. The custodian is responsible to the Board of Trustees. The office secretary does as she pleases, knows everything, and has to tell no one what she does. What matters is clarity about the preferred pattern before the minister arrives and an employment issue arises.

Office Hours. Office hours are important to specify, for they increase the effectiveness of church services to parishioners. Churches keep regular hours to benefit the parishioners. Naming those expected hours helps reinforce that purpose. Clergy need to keep hours, and they need to be free to respond to particular situations. That should be stated.

In my opinion clergy should keep regular office hours four days a week. Working on Sunday, that gives them two days to use as they see fit: personal time with the family, study-time at home, extraparochial interests.

Grievance Procedures. Some clergy think any reference to a process for handling disputes with the clergy or staff is negative thinking. On the contrary, the existence of such a system and the knowledge that it is there makes it likely that it will not have to be used. Grievance procedures are a direct consequence of statements of accountability. If a line of accountability is established, then a footnote must explain who decides if a line has been crossed wrongfully. The specification of duties makes a grievance process essential. If any party feels wronged, each knows there is a recourse.

Location and Furnishing of the Minister's Office. The minister's office is a minor matter of substance to be sure, but one with potential symbolism. If the predecessor was much loved, it is likely that the place where you work will be known as "Ken's office," but it is not. It is yours. The terms of the contract may specify your right to select and furnish an office in the church. That may mean you just move into Ken's office as is or that you pick an entirely new spot with quite different decor. It is only important that an understanding about who has the right to do what, is struck in advance.

Miscellaneous. Some ministers like to have minor matters mentioned in writing. But if they wish them mentioned, they may not be minor after all. For instance, a line about the minister's family may be in order. Or a line about the minister's extraparochial interests may be desired, especially if you come to your new pastorate with some continuing responsibility of a nonecclesiastical nature.

Empowerment. Terms of call usually contain the date they were authorized, a signature or two that identify the parties to the understanding, and a phrase about the time they govern. The customary phrase is *for an indefinite period of time.* Finally, they specify how they may be terminated. The church constitution may spell out the terminus of ministerial calls.

As long as this list may be, it is still only partial. As you begin your new pastorate, almost every day will include some new experience that you had not anticipated. The new minister may become confused and bewildered by a whole different set of circumstances and people who make and resolve the circumstances. It is impossible to anticipate every new circumstance you will meet. It would also diminish the fun and excitement of the new pastorate if all new things could be anticipated. But discussion of all these things and agreement on some of them is a good step forward. It really does free you to come to the new pastorate with some sense of what is expected of you and what you can rightly expect of others. Without such discussions, the first day at the new church will be spent wishing you had talked over some of these matters before you arrived!

"Congratulations, you are the new minister at our church!"

V.

Ripples: The Consequences of Decisions

She Doesn't Want to Go

"Dad, do we have to move?" The question was posed by my thirteen-year-old daughter, Ginny. The family was seated at the dinner table. "I don't want to leave my friends, my school, my room," she said, choking back the tears that were flooding her eyes. I had seen it before: Adolescent girls can cry frequently, surprisingly, and copiously.

"Ginny," I began, "our family would be incomplete without you. We all are going to leave behind people and places that have been important to us. When we get to New Town you will—"

Before I could finish the sentence she was wailing. "I am not going! I talked it over with Lu Ann, and she said

I can stay with her. If I do that, I can still be a cheerleader at school. I promise I will do my homework every night, and I will make my bed every day. Please let me stay with the Clarks. I will come visit you on holidays."

The other children are close to tears too. Betsy says she does not want to go either. Eddie says, "If Ginny stays here, so do I." They point out the special wonders of the place where they are. They have never been so enthused about local candy stores, basketball teams, and their friends before. We like it here, and we will not like it there, is the message that comes through loud and clear—and painfully and tearfully.

Margie sits there picking at her food. I know what she is thinking: She is thinking that the children are right, that we should not put them through this trauma, and that maybe we are making a mistake. She has her own list of deprivations she expects to encounter by this move: loss of job, loss of friends, loss of a role and status she had spent years developing.

I am not at my best to cope with these complaints. I have had many second thoughts since I accepted the call to New Town. I had thought the move was for the good of the whole family, and now I am wondering why I am inflicting such pain on everyone. I am wondering if I know what I am doing myself: Maybe I should just stay here, where I know so many people and they know me.

Almost by rote I say to this troubled family gathering all the good things about our new home. Each child will get something special when we make the move. I say it again as I have been saying for days. Only this time I am saying it because I do not know what else to say. I cannot cite the list of improvements with conviction. They do not want to hear it; they will not believe it. They are all thinking of what they are giving up, not what they may get.

I feel like a skunk.

The decision has been made: You are moving to New Town. The terms of the call have been agreed to, and the call itself has come. You have responded to it and told your congregation. You are now a lame duck pastor.

What Is Happening?

Your decision to move is producing ripples. Like a stone dropped in a placid pond, waves of effect are spreading across the waters of your life. For a sustained period of time your thoughts about moving have been personal and secretive. Now they are public: Their effect is social—touching family, parishioners, colleagues, and the community. Every person, every family, has a wide circle of interpersonal relationships altered dramatically by a decision to move. But the minister is not only a private person, he is a public one as well. Ministry is always shared, and those things that are corporate have a "we-ness" about them. That is painfully true of a decision to move.

The interval between the decision to move and the actual departure is a special and strange time for ministers and their families. Differing polities give different dimensions to this time frame. Sometimes it is swift; sometimes it is protracted. The length is less important than the meaning. Even in this interlude the opportunities for intentionality are present.

The interlude may be characterized by paradoxical surprises. In one sense, it is a relief; in another, it is a burden. The duplicity and secrecy with which negotiations are conducted are put behind you. That is a relief. Clergy are not comfortable hiding their thoughts. Part of their work with churches involves future planning. When one knows that one may not be a part of that future, the planning task is laborious and unproductive. But the real pain comes from the pastor's specialty, viz., to love and care for a particular people. When the pastor decides to move he decides to break off the loving and caring relationships he has had with his congregation. That hurts. The ripples of the decision spread across a congregation. The minister feels like a wretched stone that has precipitated what he has spent years avoiding.

The ripples of the decision within the minister's family are not especially unique. Every family that moves suffers the same experience. Because of the anomaly of living in the community where you work, the identity factors for the family are especially strong. Young children, for instance, find a part of their identity in their father's status within a community. When the decision to move is made, those identity clues for the family are sorely disrupted. To be known by a larger community and to be known in a particular way are very much a part of every individual member in a family. The prospect of that dissolution is painful.

And, finally, the ripples touch the inner life of the minister himself. His own identity is closely associated with his role in church and community. The severing of a pastoral relationship is the severing of a network of meanings, supports, and self-understandings. The decision to move is also a decision to reorder that network, and until it is reestablished one feels empty inside.

The cumulative effect of these ripples is that one feels empty inside and uncomfortable about relationships with others. That is the special power a decision to move has over those who make that decision.

The depiction of those ripples sounds heavy and unpleasant. But there are other ripples of a contrary nature. Simultaneously one has feelings of excitement and anticipation. That possibility of all things bright and beautiful in a new situation is clearly and abundantly present. It vies with the feelings of guilt and emptiness about the losses of the present situation.

Being Intentional About Grief

It helps a little to describe accurately what this interlude is. It is a grief process. Life presents losses all the time. That is the bad news of human existence. The good news is that there is a healing process that helps us cope with all the losses of life.

In *Good Grief,* Granger Westberg described the stages of grief within the human experience. His little book can help you know what to expect. He mentions, for instance, the dreamlike quality of the experience: One feels as if the loss cannot really be happening. Upon awakening it will be gone. Throughout the book he counsels confronting the fact of loss. We have many defenses to protect us from the pain of loss, but healing comes when the loss is confronted, the defenses are penetrated, and the readjustment to the new reality begins.

Those same principles apply to the loss of a pastorate. One must name and face that loss. In the vignette at the beginning of this chapter the family were conceiving plans to avoid their grief. Gently but firmly that family needs to express their pain and face their impending loss. The minister, too, must be candid about his feelings. If he feels like a skunk, he should say so. Talking it out is helpful; it is even more helpful if one knows what one is talking about.

Giving Gifts

Swiss psychiatrist Paul Tournier has written movingly of *The Meaning of Gifts.* He points out that gifts are the primary transactions of life: We give and receive countless little gifts in our interpersonal relationships. The gift theme is a helpful one in intentionally leaving a pastorate. It is true that one is experiencing the pain of impending loss, but that does not preclude the possibility of giving and receiving gifts as part of that experience.

In their grief, the minister and congregation are giving each other little gifts. They are giving each other the recognition that they have loved and cared for each other. If they had not, then leaving would be painless and meaningless. They give each other tears to express the depth and power of the relationship they have had. They need to give verbal gifts by which to express their mutual appreciation for joys and sorrows shared in intimate relationships. It is wrong to cut off the giving of those gifts to each other. It is good to be intentional about it. There may be a formal social occasion when minister and congregation can say publicly what they have meant to each other. Because this is a religious community, a special dimension of gift-giving can be experienced. As we name the gifts we have given each other in a pastoral relationship, we can give them back to God. In a worship service or in conversations we can find opportunities to thank God for the gifts he has given us in this relationship, for what they have meant to us and for how they will continue to sustain us in the power of remembering within the Christian fellowship.

Moving Is Good for Families

If you feel like a skunk in reference to your family's reluctance to move, say so. But you are not really a skunk: Moving is good for families. When you hear their grief and their plans for avoiding their pain, you are likely to forget one powerful truth: People, even little people, have an incredible ability to cope, and you are likely to underestimate your children's ability to cope with new situations. When you actually do move, they will adjust to the new reality quicker and better than you will.

Further, moving by its nature broadens the base of human experience. Your family will come to know more people, different people, different regions, different systems of doing things. Given that, they themselves will become more open to differences, more tolerant of deviation, more at home where their essential self is. Moving helps to mature children into adults who know they can cope in strange and new environments.

Another benefit is increased family identity. Although the family loses the identity it has taken from the community in which it has lived, its internal bonds are strengthened when it enters the new community. Until they find significant peer relationships they count heavily on the presence of other family members to be their companions. Even rival siblings are glad to have the company of someone they know. And together they discover as a family that they are more adaptable and flexible than they had thought. They do help one another; they do need one another. The big surprise is that family identity is portable. It is not dependent upon place; it is dependent upon sustained, nurturing, interdependent relationships. That is good to know.

There are very few reliable rules for raising children, and there are even fewer for when to move with children. No time is the right time and any time is the right time seem to be contradictory truths. It is not especially helpful, but it is true to say that the right time to move with children depends. It depends on the character of the children and their parents; it depends on the family's values; it depends on the quality of family life; it depends on what must be given up and what may be acquired.

One general guideline worth mentioning is that everyone needs a home. Add to that guideline this corollary: Home is where the family gathers. That may seem scant and conventional wisdom, but in the following for-instance it has immediate application. Ministers sometimes say, "I will move when my child finishes high school so that he can graduate with friends." By shallow wisdom, that is wrong on two counts. One, it is wrong because they may not have yet met the friends with whom they will graduate. We are not, any of us, forever locked into our present circle of friends. We make new friends all the time; so will your child in a new environment. Second, it is wrong because when that child returns home after high school, where will home be? If you move away from the town where he went to high school, when he goes home from college where will he go? Will he go where you formerly lived, or will he go home to you? In the long-term development of a person, children need to have one place to call home, and that's where the family is. If you wait for children to finish a stage of life, you may thrust them into new stages that make a return to the old very difficult.

Your Spouse's Loss

Ministerial spouses are very different people. (Some are men.) Because of these various patterns it is hard to say what will happen with one's spouse or how to cope with the changes. But all are affected directly by the minister's move.

Two elements are probably present: an inordinate investment in the spouse's own career, and a public role and identity that are associated with the minister. Some ministers are purposefully and willfully teamed with their spouses, sharing the work and affections of the congregations. Others are purposeful and willful in separating work from home. In either case, the spouse is intimately involved with the minister's career pattern. How deeply the spouse owns the decision to move probably affects more than anything else how the spouse will feel about having to move. The critical word here is *share.* Share the decision to move. Share the grief at leaving. Share the gifts that are given. Share the adventure of the new experiences.

As I later discuss, the early days in the new pastorate must include time and circumstances for husbands and wives to be together in the new environment. The sheer calamity of moving household goods should be shared: Packing and unpacking are not a private exercise. Setting up a new household requires many hands. Further, it is good work and joins you together in establishing a home in a new location.

Finally, Brethren
Before you leave your present pastorate you need to do some things for your successor. You need to make a clear break. Do not come back to your former parish

without your successor's invitation to do so. You release and relinquish the covenantal bonds when you resign. Stick to that relinquishment.

Clean your files. Do not prejudice your successor's mind about persons or decisions. On the other hand, leave critical factual information to help him become oriented in the church. You need not tell him not to sit on Mrs. Smith's overstuffed chair; he will find that out for himself. On the other hand, tell him where the Communion service is stored.

The ripples of leaving a pastorate are not to be denied or minimized. Grieve for your losses. Give and receive the gifts of shared moments. Bundle the family together, and with tears in your eyes move on.

VI

Plan B: What to Do When You Begin a Pastorate

An Evening at the Parsonage

Friends, it is good to have you here in our home. Margie and I want to become personally acquainted with you and have begun by inviting you all here in small groups.

I appreciate the way all of you told the story of your relationship to this church. It is very clear that this church has meant a lot to all of you, in very different ways. I also had you tell me what you liked best about this church so that as I begin my ministry among you I know what you think is worth preserving and strengthening. Your comments about what we need to do that we are not now doing will also be helpful to me as I begin to develop a series of recommendations to the church council about our future.

Plan B: What to Do When You Begin a Pastorate

Now, I want a chance to tell you a little bit about me. Most people do not know their ministers very well, and each of us is very different. Although I admire Ken Seim very much, I am not he. And I want you to know who I am and how you might want to use me as your minister.

I have been a pastor for fifteen years in two previous pastorates—one in Ohio and one in New Jersey. Before that I went to college for four years, and then seminary for four years. In the process of going to school I had many odd jobs: short-order cook, truck driver, and salesman to mention a few.

The one thing I most like to do in the ministry is preach. I spend a lot of my time in preparation for Sunday's sermon. I like to study in my office at the church, and I try to keep my mornings clear for that. Of course, it doesn't always work out that way. I also like teaching and counseling and do quite a bit of both. My special hobby is writing. I have had a number of articles published, and I spend much of my free time—when I am not with the family—at the typewriter.

I am sure you understand that it is impossible for any one person to do equally well all the different tasks of ministry. The one that I least like to do is visit people. I know Ken was good about that, but I have just never made that a high priority in my ministry. But I do promise you this: If you ever have need of me, want to see me, or talk to me, just let me know. That will become a high priority for me. The best way to let me know you want to see me is to call the church office and make an appointment. That is better than telling my wife or telling me when I shake hands at the door on Sundays (I am often confused as I do that) or just assuming I know you want to see me. I am not clairvoyant.

I consider it a very high honor to have been selected as your pastor. This church has a fine tradition, and you have been blessed with good and competent ministers. I will try my very best to preserve that tradition and to continue the high standard of ministry in this church.

Now, we have a bite of dessert that you might enjoy as we chat together.

Well, you have arrived. Here you are in New Town. Is it time to begin? No, it is too late for that. The time to begin is before you arrive.

You need to think first. Think of what you want to accomplish in your ministry here. Think what you want to accomplish in your first year. Think of a design that will help you meet the first year's goal. Think of what you ought to do first.

Before specific thoughts on these questions pour out, let us recapitulate the central theme of this book: a call for an intentional beginning to a new pastorate. We are trying to think of ways in which a new pastorate does not just happen but meets an objective of worth. We want to establish a pastoral relationship that will endure and enable both of us to grow. The means to do that is constant negotiation—in the larger sense of that term—and the building of trust. Trust grows as we become acquainted with one another. You have a special role and opportunity to teach this congregation about ministers in general and you in particular.

Given that background, a plan for the first year begins to emerge. During the first year we want to become acquainted as minister and people. That will preempt all other desires and designs. Those will have to wait. It will also shape whatever we do together during this first year. So, the objective before us is to design a first year that helps us get acquainted so that trust grows; so we can continually negotiate a lasting relationship of growth.

Give Yourself Some Time and Space

You need to think those thoughts. But, in the meantime, there is work, physical work, to be done. We are not turtles; we cannot carry our houses on our backs. The penalty is moving. That is sheer hard work for everyone.

A really good idea is to arrive in New Town with two weeks at your disposal before you begin work. Those two weeks can be terrific.

First, they will give you time to get settled in your new home. You and your spouse can work together unpacking, arranging, and sharing the experience of setting up a new home. Further, you can take the kids to school yourself on their first day. You can introduce them to their teachers. You can even promise to be right outside the door when school is out. Boy, does that reduce those first-day anxieties!

Not only will you help preserve the family's continuity by your presence, but you can tend to some personal business. You and your spouse can do that business together: Open checking and savings accounts, establish credit at the local stores you will be trading at, take your driver's license test, make the deposits with the utility companies, etc. It is great to have the time just to do that and, even better, doing it with your spouse seals the fact that together you are establishing a new home in this place.

If the town or the neighborhood is conducive to doing so, take a long walk through the town. You will see things this first time you may never see again as you buzz by in the car in a hurry. Walking in New Town may help you think about the ways you can establish a trust relationship in this first year.

There are some important arrangements you need to make. Establish your family with a local doctor and dentist. (The search committee may want to make some suggestions on that.) What drugstore will you trade at? What grocery store? Which gas station? There are many choices, and this is a good, relaxed time to make them.

There is some intentional learning you can do during these first two weeks. The best learning will come on Sunday. Go to the church where you will be preaching shortly. Worship with the congregation. Do that inconspicuously—arrive late, leave early. Do not tell anyone you are coming. Visiting as a worshiper the church to which you have been called gives you some essential data that you may never have another chance to gather. Find out the forms of worship they use. Find out what the pews feel like. Where is the benediction given, and does the minister greet at the door? You may never again be a part of the worshiping community as you will on that day you visit your own church.

There are also some intentional visits you can make. Do not make these incognito, make them as the brand-new minister. Visit the superintendent of schools; find out what he thinks are the strengths and weaknesses of the public school system in New Town. Visit the city manager or mayor. What can he tell you about the political structure of the communuity that you need to know? By all means, visit with the chief of police; if he will, he can tell you what really goes on in that town. Meet the funeral directors; find out what customs and traditions are followed in town at the time of death.

If possible, visit the judicatory office nearest you. You should discover the resources there, and you may want to look over its library and audiovisual resources. If the judicatory official is in, make a courtesy call. He may want to tell you about the ministerial fellowship in your area or have you find out about the health insurance program in the judicatory.

The last thing to do in these two weeks is unpack your books for your new office. You have needed the time and space for personal and familiar things. You will turn to professional matters when you begin to put your books away. It is the symbol that the new pastor has moved in.

A Thought Grows

When a new pastor arrives at a church, he has one great urge that must be resisted: He wants to jump right in and start fixing things in the church. After all, that is why they called him, isn't it? A surge of energy comes with the stimulus of a new location.

This is precisely a time when intentionality must work. You need to resist that urge to jump in. You do not know enough about the church; they do not know enough about you. Furthermore, if the church has problems that it hopes you will eventually fix, stop and think what that means. By definition, a problem has a history. If it could have been fixed, it would have been, long ago. In addition, if you should by dint of hard and imaginative work fix a church's problems, what have you really accomplished? All you have done is return everything to the status quo. That is not good enough. You need to take the long-range view. Remember, you have come here to establish a lasting relationship of mutual growth. How does running around like a whirling dervish in the first few weeks move you closer to that intentional goal? Your early energies may deter you from your long-term goal of mutual growth.

Slow down. Take it easy. You are going to need that energy later, when it will do some good. Use your mind, not your physical energy, in these first days. Be guided by your intentions, not your visceral will. You may spot instantly something you believe must be changed. Do not change it, but note it for future reference.

Here is a way to control your inclinations to jump in and start working on problems. At the first meeting of the official board ask the presiding officer to give you time on the agenda to introduce a resolution. Let that resolution have two parts. For your part as the new minister you will pledge not to make any changes in the functioning of this church; if an intractable emergency appears (the church burns down), you will consult with committees about changes. Second, for their part, the primary officers, board, and committees pledge to receive from you a series of recommendations about the future of their church. In other words, the status quo remains as it has been until the officers receive your recommendations.

There is power in that approach, though no magic power in the length of time governing the covenant. One year seems best because it will give you a chance to see all aspects of the church program as it unfolds in the course of a year. If you cannot wait that long or you think the necessity for change is critical, make the time shorter. But do stick to the terms of the agreement.

This is especially helpful in churches where there is a customarily long interval between ministers. The reason? The long interval causes lay people to say over and over, "We will wait on that until the new minister comes." What builds up is a false and high expectation of how it will be when the new minister comes. I doubt you will ride into town on the back of a donkey proclaiming the kingdom of God is at hand. If you do, you have a messiah complex, and disappointment and frustration are surely in your future.

Understand what you have done by your covenant. First, you have boxed yourself in; your hands are tied. You told the church no changes, and you violate your word at great peril. Second, you have committed the church to a planning process. What a terrific idea! You gain two important pluses, and in exchange all you gave up is some time. Do not worry about the loss of time. If there really are problems, they will be there next year too. Stick to both parts of that plan: Make no changes, and make lots of notes to yourself for the next year.

Celebrating Your Arrival

What are you going to do with all that energy and enthusiasm stimulated in you by the new situation? The heart of the church—its worship, its organization, its program—has been slowed by your agreement, and now what will you do? Why not have a party? Better yet, have a series of parties. Use some of that energy in festive occasions.

This is a serious idea: Have a party or parties. Be intentional about the celebrative mode as you begin your new ministry.

As a new pastor here are some things you need to be reminded of. Number one: The congregation are glad you are there. It is true they are anxious about who you are and what you will do to the church they love. But they heaved a small sigh of relief and said a small prayer of gratitude when you arrived. Given the tradition of churches, a church without a minister is a train without an engineer. The engineer does not move the train himself, but he knows what to do to make it go. Even before they know who you are and what you will do, they are glad to have you in their midst. Few people move into a new community with such corporate gladness for their arrival. See if you can make something of that positive fact.

Furthermore, new ministers do not come to new churches every day. It is a relatively rare experience. The atypical nature of beginning a pastorate says that it ought to be marked in some atypical way. Why not a great celebration? Why not have a special party? Maybe this event is like a birthday.

Now the question before you is how churches celebrate, or, more specifically, How does *this* church celebrate?

You may have to make some guesses. It is probably a good guess that they celebrate at morning worship. Does not your tradition have some ecclesiastical ceremony that installs or commissions a new pastor? Why not make that ecclesiastical ceremony a special time to remember?

Think about the possibilities of a worship ceremony that is very special. Would this be a good time to invite a guest preacher of special renown? Is this the time to supplement the organ with brass instruments? Is this the time to have the choir work on some special music? Is this the time to use some special symbols of ministry—the investment of a pulpit robe, a Bible, a staff of office? Is this the time to do away with the usual dreary bulletins and design a smashing cover for this service? Hey, why not do the cover on four different colored papers? Yes, this is the time and those are some of the ways. What a great celebrative service you could design. It will be a day to remember. Everyone will want to be there for that service.

Churches celebrate in worship, but how else do they celebrate? You know who really loves parties? Kids do. Why not have a party for every age in the church school? Let them meet the new minister at a party. Maybe the little kids want to play games and the older kids want to dance and put on skits. What could be a better way to meet the new minister than at a special party for you!

Maybe the rest of the congregation would feel slighted if they knew the kids were having all the fun. What about a party for older people? Does your church have many members who have belonged to it for more than forty or fifty years? Why not have a tea and reception for that very special group of people? They would be both surprised and flattered that in this church, longevity of service is noticed.

The church exists in a community; its minister is a public figure. Can this church celebrate its new minister's arrival with a community party? The congregation wants the whole town to know they are glad you have come. What is a specialty of this church that it could give to the whole town? Is it music? How about a special concert on a Sunday afternoon for the whole town? Is it art? Then how about an exhibition in the church halls? Is it arts, crafts, cookery? Why not have a country fair for everybody on the lawn?

A new minister in town takes his place among professional colleagues. There are pastors of his own denomination and pastors in the community of differing traditions. Clergy may be too stuffy to admit they went to a party for the new minister. So call it something else; call it a convocation. Make it a one-day or even a half-day workshop. Your nearby denominational seminary may have some fascinating teachers who would love to lecture a group of practicing parish ministers. Why not have a convocation on the ministry, using the resources of seminary or denominational specialists? Let it be the church's little gift to their new minister's colleagues.

Party. Party. Party. How is your energy level holding up now? Are you having fun? Are you glad you came?

Meeting the People

The single most important thing you will do that first year is meet the congregation. You will meet them any old way or by intention. You can meet them in a way that gives you an opportunity to find out not only who they are but where they are. You need an intentional plan to get acquainted with people in such a way that a trust relationship is begun. In other words, how you meet them is as important as just meeting them.

By far the best way to meet your congregation is to have them into your new home in small groups. That is an enormous undertaking that requires the full cooperation of your family. There are good reasons for having the events in your home. First, if your home is the parsonage, the parishioners are entitled to see the inside. (And the invitation method is preferable to the snoopy drop-in.) If you have purchased your own home, parishioners are curious about what you got. But there is even more: Clergy are usually treated by their congregations in ways similar to the ways clergy treat them. If your invitation to them communicates warmth and openness, that is likely to be the way they will treat you.

If it is not possible to have people into your home, then do it in one of the rooms of the church. One of the lay committees should take responsibility for the logistics. You and your spouse do not know the people well enough to handle the organization of several hundred people.

The vignette at the chapter's beginning suggests one possible format for the gathering. Maybe you want to call these "An Evening at the Parsonage." People need to know in advance that the purpose of the evening is to meet the minister and for him to become better acquainted with them. You can design the evening in any way that facilitates your purpose in having the evening. This book says the purpose is to find out where people are and to teach them about the ministry. To those ends the following components make sense.

Give people a chance to tell their own story. One way to keep this from going on too long is to pass a three-minute egg timer along: Each has until the sand runs out to tell his or her story. A better way is to be the model. Either you or your spouse shows the group how to tell the high points of their story in a succinct way by doing it first. Second, you may want to go around the group, inviting people to tell what they like best about their church or what they would like to see improved. Keep your ears open during this session. You will learn much if you hear and remember what they say. Then, an essential part of the evening is to tell them about yourself: how you got to be a minister, your education and experience, what you like best, and what you are least fond of doing. You may want to be very specific about how they can use you best. It is important to share food during the evening. There is something about sharing food that binds people in fellowship.

If that format will not work for you, you need to find another vehicle to accomplish the same end. You may want to write an essay and distribute it to the whole congregation. You may want to preach a series of sermons on the ministry. Whatever your means, you must teach them about yourself and what you do and expect from them. The surprising truth is that parishioners are very interested in what you have to say. It is likely that no one has ever sat and talked with them about ministry. What they know is based on conjecture and hearsay. You need to set them straight as far as your personality is concerned.

There are other elements to the plan to meet the congregation. For instance, you may want to extend an invitation to meet people at their work. There often exists a sharp division between home and work, and the church is clearly in the home quadrant. If you think that gap ought to be bridged, a good way to start building is to express interest in what they do. You will be edified by and appreciated for taking the time to learn about another's work.

A very important group for you to meet early is the church staff. These persons will be your co-workers. When you begin your ministry, talk to each staff member in private, maybe at a luncheon. Get them to tell you their story. Hear how they came to work for the church and how they like it. If your mind is made up and if negotiations have clarified your relationship to the staff, you may want to reiterate that position. The staff conversations establish communication links. These people are the most threatened by you. You might want to fire them all! So it is reassuring to know that the new minister is someone they can talk to. Have them define their jobs to you as they understand them. Be sure to ask them what they expect from you; that is the key question. And hear what they say.

If pastoral calling is your forte, then do it intensively when you first arrive. But beware: What people come to expect, they will want to see continued. A call to their homes may be the most important way to get to know your parishioners. If you can do it, keep ringing those bells.

Keep Faith with the Process

What has been described here is, in truth, only the beginning. It is a good intentional beginning. You must deliver whatever you have led people to believe about you. You can begin a ministry by intentionally building trust, but you cannot live off that trust forever. You must continually work at trust-building.

In the first year keep the promise you made to the official board. When the time has passed, do be ready to make your recommendations about the future of the church. A new broom does sweep clean, but a broom in the hands of one who has surveyed and well knows the territory sweeps even better.

Keep the terms of the call. If you were granted time and money for continuing education, then take it. If you agreed to certain·office hours, keep them. What you do not use or what you do not keep will in time be taken away.

Do be very visible in that first year. Show up for all church activities. You may want to remark that you do not expect to be present at every church event, but at the beginning you want to see and learn everything you can about this church.

A Final Word to the Pastoral Search Committee

A good pastoral search committee deserves a good conclusion. Tie up the loose ends before you disband. Do communicate to the congregation. Remind them that the new minister is not like the former minister. If the minister has told you some of his hopes about beginning his pastorate, do pass those along to the congregation. Make sure that all the written agreements and the basic understandings that exist between you and the minister are in the hands of the proper person for further disposition. Report to the denomination what actions you have taken.

Help the new minister feel welcome in his new home. Remember, you are the only persons in the new church that he knows. See that the parsonage is ready for him. Let him know how eager you are for him to begin life among you.

But most of all, brag about what a terrific job you did. Tell anyone who will listen that you deliberately searched for just the right person. Say how fortunate you are to have found that right person. Spread abroad the skills he brings to this ministry. In this particular case it is not only all right to brag, it helps the new minister begin in an expectant climate. Besides, you deserve congratulations. You did your best, and a good match has been made. Long may it live!

VII

Stoles: Learning the New Works of Ministry

Preface to the First Sermon

You see before you a solitary figure. My face and voice are unfamiliar. I am a newcomer to this church and this community. It is said of me that I am the new minister.

But look closely; look with the eyes of faith. I am a solitary figure, but I am a representative figure. I stand before you with a cloud of witnesses. In my person, many kind and wise and loving people have shared their lives with me, and a bit of them lives in me. In my profession I share an honorable tradition: I share the ministry of Christ with the whole church; I share my ordination with colleagues known and to be made known to me; I share the historic faith with the saints and the apostles. I dare not stand here alone to speak the Word of God to you, but in the company of so many I am made bold to speak the Word as the Spirit gives me utterance.

The strangeness of my face and voice is a temporary condition. Even now, as you see and hear me, I am moving from anonymity to personhood. In the tomorrows to come we shall share ceremonies, festivities, and occasions to discover who we are in this pastoral relationship. You do not need me; you need the spirit of Christ to animate your bones and swell your spirit. I cannot do that for you. But it is the testimony of scripture that where we meet in need, the spirit of Christ dwells there.

It is true that I am a newcomer to this church and community, but in that I share a common experience; once you were new to this place. You have made a home here; so shall I. You have become a participant in this community of faith; so shall I. You have grown to love one another and care for others' joys and sorrows; so shall I. As we walk together in faith, time will banish the memory of when we joined the pilgrimage.

I am your new minister, duly called to be so by the traditions of our church. I have come here leaving a grieving people, and grieving myself for the losses my family and I have borne in our departure. I have come to a people grieving for the loss of their former pastor. Each of us shall honor and preserve what in our past has been good. As we instill these memories in that portion of the self that abides, we also relinquish their claim upon us. We are free to be you and me. We have freely chosen to walk together. We are free to grow in the covenant and communion Christ has established in his church.

In the name of Christ we begin. The hurts and hopelessness of the world are our mission. Understanding and being understood are our fellowship. Hope in the amazing grace of God is our faith. Strangers and fixtures have in common a fellowship with Christ. Building upon that, let us begin.

This chapter is entitled "Stoles." A stole is a colorful cloth worn around the neck, symbolizing the yoke of Christ upon the wearer. Clergy sometimes wear stoles while performing the cultic rites of worship, preaching, and the sacraments.

This chapter, then, is about the functional roles of ministry as they are intentionally conceived during the first year. It cannot be said too strongly that the ways in which you begin probably will be the ways in which you continue. Be careful of which rut you pick to travel.

Intentional Preaching

Most of your congregation will meet you first in the pulpit. Their first impressions of the kind of person you are will come by experiencing your preaching. With the passage of time they will expect to have their impressions reconfirmed by hearing you speak to them from the pulpit. In the jargon of advertising, through preaching you create an image of who you are, what you believe, how you relate to people.

109

There is not much to say about your preaching style. You have been developing that over the years and will continue to do so. But there is something to be said about the intention and the content of sermons in a new pastorate.

In the first year, preaching should have your highest priority. Even if you do not like to preach, during that first year you should really work hard at the task. There are several reasons for this strong advocacy about the priorities of your time and functions. In mainline Protestantism, preaching is expected, and your congregation is also set for a person who can and does preach. Even wishing that it were otherwise will not make it so. If those expectations about your preaching are not fulfilled, the congregation will have to change its expectations of you. That can be done, but it takes time and special education to do so.

Second, the kind of preaching you do sets the tone for the rest of your ministry in this place. If you preach abrasive sermons, people may respect you, but they will hold you at some distance in personal relations. If you preach kind and gentle sermons, they may embrace you personally but have reservations about your forthrightness. The image factor is obviously working. How do you want to be perceived by your congregation? What of yourself will you reveal in your public appearance and function in the pulpit?

A third, practical reason for emphasizing preaching is that you will have more time for it during the first year than you will with the passage of time. You have undertaken an ambitious program designed to acquaint you with your congregation, and you have not been in the community long enough to accumulate the denominational and community assignments that will occupy your time. Your counseling load is lighter, and you have not yet initiated any new programs or organizational structures. Those will come, but in the first year your time is best spent on preaching.

What to Preach

Convictions about the freedom of the pulpit make it hazardous to suggest specific sermons in that first year. But the larger concept of intentional beginnings offers some guidelines. For instance, your very first sermon, the one your congregation will make a special effort to hear, may be very personal. You may want to preach on the formative religious experiences you have had. You may want to declare your approach to ministry. You may want to speak of your expectations for the church. But one of those is enough. Personal sermons are thin until the congregation really knows and trusts the person.

A sermon series, announced in advance, is a good corrective to the overly personal temptations of the first year. You may want to consider a year-long series on the basic beliefs of the Christian faith. Take one of the creeds or statements of faith, and preach about it word for word. The intention for this kind of preaching in the first year is to develop a basic vocabulary: What do we mean when we say "Jesus Christ is Lord"?

If historic creeds are not your thing, you may want to do a series of sermons on the Christian life-style. Again, you are trying to develop a common nomenclature upon which to build in the future. Stewardship, prayer, evangelism, worship, etc., are fit components in the life-style series.

Or, if you insist upon overtly biblical themes, you may want to preach a series of sermons on the ministry of Jesus as it is presented in one of the Gospels. Trace its development and its emphases as present in a particular Gospel. Here, again, such a series is intended to lift up models that you and your new congregation may want to have in mind as you negotiate the kind of ministry you want to have in this new pastorate.

Or, if your preaching style centers on exegeting pericopes from a lectionary, by all means do so. But you may want to add in the liturgy a short section on basic word studies. Perhaps only a minute or two in length, it will give you the opportunity to develop that basic vocabulary with the congregation.

Changing the Liturgy

In many churches the liturgy is the same. In others it is shaped by the custom and tradition of the local congregation. In most churches the minister is the officiant in the liturgy, but a particular lay committee has technical jurisdiction over its form.

As a new minister, you should know that you change the liturgy in a new congregation at great peril. Even if it seems to you that the liturgy is done by rote and without thought or meaning, you will be surprised at the concern expressed if you put the offering in a different place in that liturgy. Hence the importance of the suggestion to attend worship services before you become the minister. If you cannot do that, perhaps for the first month you can ask lay members to conduct the liturgy for you until you become familiar with their customs.

Changing the liturgy by means of pastoral decree is suspect, but the liturgy can be changed if you take an intentional approach in doing so. For instance, you may ask the chairperson of the lay committee charged with the liturgy to give you half an hour at each of their meetings during the year. Use that time to teach the board about worship. You may want to compare other traditions to your own. As this year-long teaching draws to a close, you may want to present this board with a new form of worship for the congregation. Make a cogent rationale for the changes you want to make. See if they will concur in trying an alternate approach to worship, and see if they will help interpret the new form to the congregation. Be willing to abandon your preferred form if strong resistance develops. Come back next time with a variation on your preferred approach.

The Sacraments and Special Services

Before a major religious festival you should consult with the lay committee about customary forms for these festivals. You will want to know that the sanctuary is bedecked with Easter lilies or that a

Christmas tree has always been next to the pulpit. You may not like these customs, but you will like even less being surprised by them. Make a note of what you consider inappropriate customs so you can include the approach you prefer in your second-year recommendations.

Baptisms, weddings, and funerals may also have local nuances. If you had a chance to visit funeral directors, as suggested earlier, then you have gathered some data on funeral customs. That is probably not possible when it comes to learning about weddings, baptisms, and Communion. In the case of weddings and baptisms look in the records and see who recently participated in those services. Go and see them, and find out what was actually done. The lay committee in charge of worship often knows what is customary in serving Communion. Plan a night with them in which you rehearse the Communion service.

Pastoral Counseling

In the new pastorate the beginnings of pastoral care are in preaching, when the congregation makes its judgments about who you are and how you relate. In the first year you will not do much pastoral counseling. It takes people a long time to decide you can be trusted.

There is one exception to that general observation. In the first year certain people will want to see you. These people are sometimes called "the emotional cripples." They are persons with perennial problems who virtually make a career of telling their troubles to others. They love to talk to ministers, who are so understanding. These people will want to see you *because* you are new. You will handle them as you think best: Be supportive or discourage them. But the point is to expect them. They live in every community.

In the first year you need to clear out your head about pastoral care. It is not the same everywhere; it changes from place to place. The first year is the time to forget what you have always done and to think about a model of pastoral care in this new place. For instance, if you were accustomed to having five weddings a year, you planned fifteen or twenty hours for premarital counseling. What will happen to you in your new pastorate if it is likely that you will have twenty-five weddings a year? When you move you have to change more than address.

If you have moved to a larger church, one of the surprises that may come upon you is that pastoral care is much less personal. In the larger church your role as pastor may be facilitating special groups of persons rather than meeting with individuals on a regular basis.

The first year is the time to establish your contacts with referral agencies. Get to know community resources for family counseling, mental health, and physical disease. You are often the first contact people make when facing a personal problem. Often your counseling role is to direct persons to the special agency that can help them. You cannot do that if you do not know the resources available. Find out what they are.

A new minister signals a fresh start for the whole congregation. You do not know recent past history; they do not know who you are. While it is important to meet each person afresh and let them become unique persons to you, the new minister should expect to encounter certain "types" of people. Expecting to meet certain types of persons is part of intentional ministry. Having those expectations is good in that it helps you to relate to them in certain pastoral ways. It is not good if you assume you already know all there is to know about these particular persons. For instance, when you meet the very old members of the congregation you are likely to hear them say—or know that if they truly spoke their minds they would say, "Well, I had expected Ken Seim to preach my funeral sermon, but now I guess I will have to get to know you." Or, at the other end of the spectrum, you will meet persons in their late twenties or early thirties who have recently returned to the church. They may have been very active in the youth group, growing up in the church, but now they will say, "It is all so different now."

What this may mean is that *you* are what is different. Persons who have been close personal friends of the former minister need special attention. It is more than likely that they feel betrayed by their good friend's leaving; they feel you are not their friend and may not likely become so. The new pastorate has many grieving faces, and in each the grief process presents

116

itself in differing ways. It may be small consolation at the moment, but the unalterable fact is that the grief process will begin again when you leave this parish. It always does. The difference is whether you are the recipient or the perpetrator of the grief.

Church Administration

If you follow the approach of chapter 6, you have virtually declared a moratorium on church administration—at least, on changes within the administrative structure. However, that does not mean church administration ceases.

You need to attend every regular meeting of all the boards and committees throughout the year. You need to know what they are currently doing.

Ask each chairperson for a half hour at their meeting. Use the time to read and discuss what the constitution says are the duties and prerogatives of this particular committee. Ask them how they perform those tasks and how those tasks relate to the overall purposes and mission of the church.

In the first year, boards and committees will want to know what you think on particular questions. As a general rule, you should back off from answering those questions. Even if you know very well what you think, as soon as you say what you think, you have closed the dialogue with those who think differently, and you have disclosed that you really do not understand the situation. Keep your mouth shut and your ears and eyes open. Keep that notebook handy.

Beginning a New Pastorate

It should be burgeoning with observations and suggestions for the next year.

Changing Your Ministry

James Glasse remarked that "if a minister says he has had fifteen years' experience, what he probably has had is three years' experience five times over." That is partly true. It is possible for ministers to learn the techniques of their craft and to go on applying them for the rest of their lives.

Intentional ministry does not allow that. It requires you to change your ministerial style as you change churches. The reason is very simple: Churches are different. To be a minister of a particular church is to shape a style of ministry appropriate to that particular church. The concept of intentional beginnings is a concept of change.

The suggestions in "Stoles" concern how you go about accepting the yoke of Christ in a new pastorate. They bid you to pause and reconceive ministry according to the dimensions of a particular church. If you jump right in and do what you have been doing, you will not change; you will merely perpetuate what you have done.

In the days of vaudeville a performer perfected his act, and once perfected only the location changed. In the television age a performer can do his act only once, then everyone has seen it. Today the performer must change his act or go out of business.

Today's ministry has similar requirements. When you move, you must change your ministry. Knowing what must be changed requires a process of discernment. Intentional beginnings is one process that provokes those discernments.

Fan Mail

It is hoped that your imagination has been stirred by the intentional process as it applies to ministerial moves. However, there is a risk in stirring the imagination: You may create fantasies.

Intentional ministry is a process, not a panacea. Even when applied fully, thoroughly, and effectively, it does not turn all frogs into princes or overcome all obstacles to life in a Christian community. Far from it. Intentionality is an alternative to chance. Intentionality as it pertains to ministerial moves is an insight into group dynamics. No one group is completely homogeneous; every group is an assembly of unique individuals. A new pastorate, like an old pastorate, is precisely that: an assembly of unique individuals bound by their loyalties to Christ and the church. Somewhere along the line an individual or two or more will miss the process, not connect with what is going on, and feel left out. That is both unfortunate and inevitable. You need to know the limits of intentionality as applied to assemblies of individuals.

To make my point I am including in this chapter two letters from my files. They disclose the painful truth of the cliché that you can't win 'em all.

Mr. Kemper:
I have been a member of First Church a long time. I have always enjoyed good relationships with the minister.

Therefore, it pains me deeply to have to write this letter. I have tried in every way I know how to keep an open mind about you. I know that each minister is different, and all have their own strengths and weaknesses. Our church has indeed been fortunate because we have had so many very fine ministers. If you do not know it already, then I must tell you myself. Two years ago I had a very serious automobile accident. (You may have noticed I still walk with a cane.) I know that I could not have survived that accident without the help of God and Ken Seim. Ken was one of the first to come to the hospital. He stayed on with my husband and children while my life literally teetered on the brink. He prayed for me all night long. After I became stable he would come to the hospital a few times a day. Later, when I began to recuperate, I looked forward to his afternoon visits. I could talk with him about so many important things. When I came home he saw to it that we had meals from the church for weeks. He stopped by the house just to see how I was doing. If I believe in God—and I do—it is because of Ken Seim. He is a godly man!

I hated it when Ken announced he was leaving. I cried and cried. I went to see him and begged him to reconsider moving. But he felt he had to leave. He felt the church needed a change and that a new minister would bring a different style and emphasis that the church needed. He asked me to give the new minister a chance to become acquainted with us. I promised him I would try.

I have tried. I have gone to church regularly. I attended all the social activities we had for you. I even went to your home. But, I must say that you are simply not the man Ken Seim is. I fear our church has made a terrible mistake. I know you are not the same as Ken Seim, but I really expect a minister to care about the congregation. I cannot understand your sermons. The "parties" were a lot of wasted time that you should have spent in teaching the children about God. You have only been to see me once because my neighbor asked you to come, and you did not even offer to say a prayer with me. This church needs a minister who cares. We need a minister who will help his people when they need it. I am truly sorry you are not that minister.

I will continue to pray for our church. Maybe God will know that you need a new church and we need another minister.

Prayerfully,
Maude Emerson

Dear Mr. Kemper:

Since you came to our church I have become aware of your high-handed ways. You manipulate this congregation! You have everything come out the way you want it to, but you make it *seem* as if we are doing what we want to do. In fact, you are pulling the strings of our boards and committees.

As a case in point, I object to the way you influenced our recent budget. For years I have believed that "charity begins at home." I can take you to many needy families within walking distance of our church. I say we should support these families first. But in our recent budget there are no funds for these; instead there is an increase of our contributions to the denomination's superchurch, one-world activities. I know you are responsible for that increase. You could at least have waited until you had been here long enough to learn about the real needs of this community and the true attitudes of your members before you went off pell-mell for some great give-away program.

To be sure, it looks as if the mission board of our church wanted it, but I am sure that you influenced their minds, just as you have tried to influence us about what a great minister you are. Well, I am one who sees through that kind of malarkey. You may fool them, but you cannot fool all of us.

A friend

VIII

Passages: When You Are No Longer the New Minister

The Minister Writes on His First Anniversary

It is surprising to note that one year ago this week I preached my first sermon to this congregation. It is surprising because I feel I have always lived here.

You have made me feel at home. In countless ways you have expressed your appreciation and support for my ministry among you. From the day we moved in with the well-stocked shelves to this day, my cup hath "runneth over." You have been charitable about the newcomer's mistakes, patient while he has found out who you are, and eager for what is yet to be. A minister dare not ask for more from a congregation.

This anniversary marks not only elapsed time, but a

new dimension in our life together. When I came here I promised the church council I would spend the first year becoming acquainted with this congregation, and at its end I would make some suggestions about our mission, informed observations, I hope, based on a year's observations and suggestions.

I am developing those recommendations right now. They will be introduced at the officer's retreat this fall, and then distributed to the whole congregation. In a real sense these are your recommendations put in my words. I have listened carefully to your hopes and dreams for this church. In the process of listening, they have become my hopes and dreams too.

Frankly, I am surprised at how many suggestions I have to put forth. If you did not know this church well, you might think we are in big trouble. Nothing could be further from the truth; we are growing stronger all the time. The sheer length of my report is evidence that we are strong. Only a growing church could entertain these possibilities. If I did not think we had enormous potential, I would say nothing of it. That I have so much to say rightly suggests a high-potential future.

I am going to do a strange thing with these recommendations. I am going to give them away. That is not as generous as it may sound; they are your thoughts in the first place. I am giving them back to you. In the processes of this church, we will weigh and consider the merits of each. Some will be rejected immediately; some will be enacted immediately —which is the question before us. I have learned to trust your wisdom in this first year. That makes it possible for me to trust your wisdom in the future.

The rites of passage are important to human beings. We have birthdays, confirmations, even funerals to mark the passages of life.

There are no rites or symbols for the passage from "new pastor" to "pastor." There are subtle signs and signals if we can discern them. When do you quit referring to your former pastorate as "back home"? When do parishioners stop giving you directions to their homes? When do your children begin to use possessive pronouns, e.g., "my" school, "our" town? When does it take you more than an hour to do your errands because people you meet on the street want to chat? There is no accurate measurement for when you pass the boundary. But you will know when it happens.

Losers and Lovers

There is a curious but certain phenomenon about the passage from "new" minister to "the" minister. You know you are the minister when something you very much want for the church gets shot down and you are still loved and respected even though a loser in this particular instance. New ministers often have their way about church decisions—a "honeymoon" phenomenon. Some new ministers are deceived by the phenomenon and think that this is indeed a different church and that they are performing a different kind of ministry. But as in a marital

124

relationship, with the passage of time you are confronted with overwhelming evidence that you will not always have your way, that conflict will develop, and—surprise—the relationship can stand the stress. Such evidence may come in the budget development for next year. You are sure that a 10 percent increase in missionary-giving will be a high priority for the congregation, and you say so at the budget meeting. But when the votes (ballots or dollars) are counted, you are wrong. It may be a gentle rebuff or even a hard slam to earth, but the clue is not so much in the event as in the response to it. The clue to the health of the relationship is whether you and the congregation can genuinely say to each other, "OK, that was a surprise, now let's see what we can work on for the long-term development of the mission program" or whatever the specific may be. It is not pleasant to lose, but it may be a small comfort to know that when the congregation can say no and still hold you in affection, it is a sure sign that you are on your way to being the minister and not just the new kid on the block.

The Process Never Ends

Peter Drucker declares that "effective management consists of creating new tasks." That speaks of an anticipatory style of leadership. Part of your first year in the parish is spent anticipating the second. To be sure, there needs to be periodic review. How are we doing on our goals? Should they be revised based on new data? Sometimes the review suggests abandonment. Churches are very poor at abandoning that which has been begun and lives on in dwindling importance. But more important than review and abandonment is the creation of new tasks. What is and what might be are the bifocal vision of effective ministry.

Renegotiating

Negotiation is never a once-and-for-all experience. It goes on and on. Churches, I have said repeatedly, are voluntary organizations. They grow on trust. Trust is an elusive estate: Just when you think it is secured it dissolves, and just when you think it has vanished it emerges in strength and in power. Clergy must do their part in keeping that trust growing. They know they are trustworthy, but they forget congregations are processions and that a parade of persons passes through the doors. In time what has been established slips but can be reestablished. A systematic accounting of your stewardship of the ministerial office is a necessity. You need to do it; the congregation needs you to do it. They need to know what you are doing, thinking, and planning.

Gratitude

You cannot say thank you to the congregation often enough. Gift-giving is the metaphor of pastoral relationships. Love, hope, faith, and trust are reciprocally given and received in pastorates. They should not leave you speechless or prayerless. That churches exist, given the tenuousness of human relationships, suggests divine creation and governance.

The Next Pastorate

The next pastorate may be the one you are at. So powerful is intentionality and the negotiating process that you can, in the course of time, change your role without changing your location. The ability to do that fulfills the intention with which we began, viz., to develop a lasting relationship of mutual growth.

However, if a change of location seems desirable in the course of time, you will not be the same person who makes the change. You have learned so much more about churches and ministry that the next move will be different. If you have learned nothing, you will repeat what you have always done. Mistakes, when repeated, become patterns requiring defense and justification. Intentional ministry is never a pattern, rather a process. It enables you to live with freedom and tradition, enhancing the power of both.